SIX OF ONE
HALF DOZEN OF ANOTHER

Twelve Stories about Family, Indiana Kidhood and Other Goofy Stuff

MIKE REDMOND

Guild Press
Emmis Publishing, LP

SIX OF ONE HALF DOZEN OF ANOTHER
All rights reserved.
Copyright © by Mike Redmond

GUILD PRESS EMMIS PUBLISHING, LP
10665 Andrade Drive
Zionsville, Indiana 46077

The Guild Press website address is
www.guildpress.com

ISBN 1-157860-113-4
Libraryof Congress Catalogue Card Number 2002107993

Text and layout design by April Altman Reynolds
Cover design by Lloyd Brooks, Thrive, Inc.

Printed and bound in the United States of America

For my family—
past, present and yet to be.
You know who you are. And so do the authorities.

~ Foreword ~

Let us be blatant right up front, shall we? Thank you for buying Mike Redmond's first book. Read it. It's good for you.

This work is a glorious salutation to family and kidhood, Mike's term, and all they entail.

Allow me to tell you what *Six of One, Half Dozen of Another* is to me.

For starters, it's just like sitting in an apple crate while riding around Catskill, New York, in Papa's delivery truck, *circa* 1959, dropping packages for Lerners New Department Store.

It's also like flying through a plate-glass window during *Superman* rehearsals in Columbus, Ohio, a few years later or sitting as a family on the drop-down tailgate of a 1960 Chevrolet station wagon, marveling at Columbus' Fourth of July parade.

I'm certain it also is hanging out in front of a cranky black-and-white TV, trying to dial in *Huckleberry Hound* early on a Saturday morning, and making "Today's Specials" with my brother. (For the uninitiated, "Today's Specials" are wrought by slathering two Ritz crackers with Skippy peanut butter, adding one major glop of Smucker's grape jelly and then trying to load the whole nine yards into your mouth before the jelly squirts out onto the carpet in the den. It's served with warm Coca-Cola, right out of the glass bottle with the chipped paint on it—only because we couldn't reach the ice-cube trays in the freezer. Delightful and refreshing, "Today's Specials" were the fortified start to any Saturday back then.)

It's all about the exhilaration associated with our home being packed with relatives and presents (presents, we LOVED presents) for special occasions. Or the first trip to Niagara Falls, or, for that matter, the drive down the Pacific coastal highway, which nearly caused Dad a nervous breakdown (not because of the cliff-laden drive, but because his young teenage sons were bickering so mightily that one sat up front with him—that would be me—the other in the back with Mom. The Scotch tab that night probably necessitated a major reconfiguration of the trip budget. Sorry, folks.)

It's about testing the invention of the Wham-O Super Ball on the patio, seeing whether it indeed could, with simply one bounce, arc over the roof and land in the front yard—or in Mrs. Powers' living room across the street. (It could … on both accounts.)

Above all else, for me, this book is about the warmth and bond my family shares, the ups and downs we've encountered, the love we accorded each other—and still do today, thankfully.

See, all this recollection and reflection stems from my kidhood. I owe the author a debt of gratitude for reconnecting me to it. You'll feel similarly, I'm certain, when you finish reading the book. You're about to embark on a warm and blissful read. If that seems sappy to you, I'm sorry. It made me feel good. What can I say?

With masterful insertions of humor, Mike takes you on a journey that is, above all else, a magnificent celebration of family, and the Platinum Age of life: kidhood.

You'll find yourself laughing—not necessarily aloud, as you would when reading one of his award-winning humor columns, because this isn't about the knee slap. You'll smile, and you'll do it broadly. You may even drop a tear or two; he can be poignant, you know.

Wait! Before you do the "thumb thing" to Chapter One, you first must understand the author. He is not a simple man, and that's a good thing. You'll find him right at the top of my Friendship Food Chain. This man I call Red is as loyal, insightful, intellectual and certainly as witty as anyone whom I've had the pleasure to come to know. He's that guy, the one in the red-flannel shirt with the Pall Mall dangling from his lips, standing in the hallway outside the City Room of *The*

Indianapolis News, The (Late) Great Hoosier Daily, espousing the virtues of perfect softball pitching form and Dweezil Zappa's rise to music fame in the same conversation.

He can tell you everything about the Oliver 77 tractor—and I mean everything. He can speak to you in Russian. He can make all manner of stringed instruments tap dance, and has a profound depth of knowledge of music and the people who perform it, and his CD collection dwarfs that.

In addition, he knows every line from *Blazing Saddles* and the intrinsic worth of a fine bologna sandwich and root beer lunch. (Can YOU reel off a fair chunk of the Preamble to the Constitution during a righteous root beer belch?)

He can tell you anything you want to know about ice hockey; heck, he can stand next to you, all choked up, in the full-scale replica of the Montreal Canadiens' dressing room, the one from The Forum, at the Hockey Hall of Fame in Toronto, reciting the names of the All-Stars who wore the famed sweaters of *Les Habitantes.* (Still, they don't compare to the Detroit Red Wings of his kidhood, or of today for that matter, in Red's mind.)

The boy can cook, too. Just be sure to remain clear of the kitchen when he's on task. You can count Cuban and German among his areas of great culinary command.

He's incredibly well read. He does several newspapers a day, dozens of books a year and various Internet sites—seemingly simultaneously.

He's a first-rate uncle to his nieces and nephew and a superlative pseudo-uncle to my daughters, who comfortably refer to him as Uncle Red.

At the core, though, my dear friend Red is a skillful writer. That's what he does. He works vigorously to tell stories and somehow finds a way to make you a part of them—and that's precisely what he has achieved with respect to the book you're holding in your hands.

With this tome, Red has taken me back to places I hadn't revisited in years (and years). It will do the same for you. I swear it will, just as I swear (note crossed index and middle fingers behind back) I had nothing, absolutely nothing, to do with the missing Bazooka bubble gum and Lik-M-Aid packets from Cooper's Drug Store back in '63.

Steve Greenberg
Carmel, Indiana
May 12, 2002

·~ Beginnings. ~·

The stories you are about to read are true. Well, mostly. The names have not been changed to protect the innocent because as near as I can tell, no one in my family fits that description . . .

For me, it begins in Peru, Indiana. That's Miami County. I know a lot of people think I am a native of LaGrange County, the little place up by the Michigan line, because I've written so much about it. The fact, however, is that my family moved there when I was thirteen. Although I think of LaGrange County as home, and tell people I'm from there, I am not an actual born-and-bred LaGrange Countian . . . Countier . . . Countizen. Whatever. I was raised there but not born there, so don't call me a LaGrange County native. After all, if your cat moved her kittens into the oven, you wouldn't call them biscuits.

Now, although I was not born in LaGrange County, I do have some credentials there. My mother was a LaGrange County native, as were her parents and their parents before them. Our family roots run deep into the sand and muck that pass for LaGrange County soil. People who might not have known me personally knew that I was part of a large, respected and old LaGrange County family, and tended to cut some slack, grease the skids, give me a break. Being the grandson of Nathan and Marion McKenzie was of immeasurable help to a non-biscuit like me, especially when I was a teenager and somewhat inclined toward occasional interaction with the civil authorities, such as school administrators or the LaGrange County Sheriff's Department. The family honor remained unsullied. Besides, those records were sealed.

Of my parents' four children, only one of us was LaGrange

County-born, and that was kind of a fluke. Vicky decided to make her entrance while Mom was visiting Grandma and Grandpa. Had she waited, she could have been born in Bloomington, where Dad was attending Indiana University, but Vicky never was long on patience.

I came along four years later when Dad was working as a sportswriter and photographer at *The Peru Tribune*. My brother P.D.—Patrick Dennis, in case you wondered—was born in Indianapolis, two years and change later, when Dad was working at *The Indianapolis News*. The baby of the family, Amy, was born nine years after P.D., in Bethesda, MD. By that time Dad was out of the newspaper business entirely and working for a congressman. Good thing. It paid more, and four kids ranging from age sixteen to newborn will vacuum the money right out of a wallet.

So there you go: four kids born in four places, only one of them LaGrange County, and that more or less by accident. And the kicker is no two of us have the same color hair or eyes. Vicky's hair is dark brown (or used to be) and her eyes are brown, too. My hair is somewhat lighter and my eyes are hazel. P.D.'s hair is lighter than mine and he has green eyes. Amy is a blue-eyed blond. This used to lead to jokes about four kids being born in four different places by four different milkmen. For some reason neither Dad nor Mom thought that was particularly funny. We kids thought it was a riot.

The beginning of my memory is in Indianapolis, in a duplex on Brookside Parkway, North Drive. Specifically, I remember the wood inlay of the staircase landing coming up to meet me as I fell down the stairs. And as beginnings go, even for memory, it's not exactly auspicious.

You see, the reason the landing was coming up to meet me (and quite rapidly, as I recall) is that I was trying to walk around in a pair of my mother's high heeled shoes. I think they were beige, if that matters to you. It does to some people. Every time I mention getting clobbered while wearing my mother's high heels, some joker wags his eyebrows suggestively and asks what color they were. Come on. I was three years old. I knew nothing about cross-dressing or fetishes. Also, since I most likely was wearing a pair of Billy-the-Kid jeans and a T-shirt, it would seem that I also knew nothing about accessorizing.

My tumble down the stairs did lead to another beginning, though: that of my association with newspapers. You see, when I fell face-first onto the landing, I gave myself my first, and perhaps best, black eye. I mean, it was a lulu—purple and green and yellow, completely encircling my left eye—the sort of shiner that makes people draw back in admiration. *My Lord*, they say to themselves, *what a stout young man he is, being able to take such a wallop*. Which, of course, is what you want them to think.

My Dad, enterprising young newsman that he was, saw an opportunity. He set up his lights and camera, dressed me in a pair of ratty old underpants, put boxing gloves on my hands and took my picture.

Two days later my picture appeared in *The Indianapolis News* with a caption about how I forgot to duck and demanded a rematch. It said nothing about falling down the stairs while wearing my mother's shoes. I guess that was another beginning: the beginning of my understanding that when you're going for laughs, you have to leave out certain details.

The day after that, I received a letter from Reddy Kilowatt, the little electric-bolt guy who was the mascot of the Indianapolis Power and Light Company, wishing me a speedy recovery. This goes to show you that it was a different world back then. If it happened today, chances are Mom and Dad would have gotten the letter, and it would have been from Child Protective Services. I'm sad to say I understand it completely, too. Too many kids out there are sporting black eyes for reasons far uglier than falling down a half-flight of stairs wearing their mothers' beige pumps. It breaks your heart.

But that's not what this is about. Sorry. I get sidetracked sometimes. Where were we? Oh, yes. Beginnings.

I began school in Indianapolis and loved it from the first moment. It was kindergarten. We sang, played, drank juice and took naps. What was not to love?

I didn't get to love it very long, though, because I came to kindergarten with another beginning already under my belt: I had begun to read.

It happened quite by accident. My mother, you see, is a finger reader. She traces her index finger down the page, under the line she is reading. She did this as she read to me, and it didn't take much work on my part to figure out that her finger was pointing to the word she was saying. By the time I went into kindergarten at age five-going-on-six, I already had two years of reading under my belt.

I was, of course, fond of the classics: Little Golden Books. Anything by P. D. Eastman. My big sister's hand-me-down Little Red, Green and Blue Books—the ones with Tom, Betty and Susan instead of Dick and Jane. We Tom-Betty-Susan people, in fact, think Dick and Jane are highly overrated. Tom, Betty and Susan—now THERE was some thrilling reading. "See Tom run. Run, Tom, run!" Talk about a page-turner.

So after a few weeks of kindergarten, I was sent—reluctantly—to the first grade. I say reluctantly because Vicky had already briefed me about what to expect in the true academic world: no more play, no more juice, no more naps. First grade meant getting down to business, and I didn't like the idea one bit. I really enjoyed that juice.

I swam in the academic tide with the rest of the minnows until I got to fourth grade, when it was determined by testing that I was of above-average intelligence (their mistake; what I had was a knack for taking tests) and should be sent to another school where I could be in a classroom of people like me, the very thought of which frightens me now that I see it in print. So away I went from the friendly confines of George S. Buck Elementary School #94 to the great unknown, Floro Torrence Elementary School #83, which, of course, is a difference of eleven numbers.

This was the beginning of a stretch in which I found myself going through schools like an Army brat, which, of course, I was not. I was just a regular brat in unusual circumstances. But I was a regular brat who had to find his way to the boys' room and learn who to watch out for in the cafeteria just about every year. I went to different schools in fourth, fifth, sixth, seventh, eighth and tenth grades. Even so, I thought Vicky had it tougher. She went to three different high schools in the same stretch. She had to learn three different fight songs and join three different Spanish clubs.

In the end, though, we wound up in LaGrange County, a little square of real estate in northeastern Indiana known chiefly for its large Amish population, the flea market in the town of Shipshewana, and the sixty-four natural lakes created when the last glacier rolled through the area. None of which figured very much in my kidhood, except maybe the lakes. The Amish are concentrated on the west side of the county. Our family is from the east side. The flea market is a tourist deal. And the lakes—well, I fished and swam in a couple of them, of course, but they were little ones up in the northeastern part of the county, near our home. The "big" lakes, the ones where people from Fort Wayne and Indianapolis have their summer cottages, where their kids water-ski and have names like "Chip" and "Sissy" who make fun of us locals—those are down by Wolcottville, in the southern part of the county. I didn't get down there much.

My life centered on the farm where my grandparents lived. Grandma and Grandpa McKenzie had thirteen children (Halcyon, Ardelle, Van, John, Nelta, Eldon, Bruce, Mildred, my mother Lois, Dean, Margaret, Verl and Sharon) who in turn produced fifty grandchildren (if you think I am going to name them here, you're crazy). Their farm was the hub of the McKenzie wheel, and weekends would usually find no fewer than three families gathered there eating, laughing, talking, playing, working.

Seldom were we all there at the same time. In fact, the only time I can remember all thirteen of Grandma and Grandpa's children being there, with all their spouses and all their children, was the old folks' fiftieth wedding anniversary in 1967. That was mammoth. Families were billeted in four houses—Grandma and Grandpa's, Uncle John and Aunt Mary's, Uncle Maurice and Aunt Nelta's, ours. We ate in shifts and slept on floors like litters of puppies. For a kid, it was glorious. Having all my cousins around meant that I could always find someone to do something with—play Monopoly or baseball, climb trees, shoot BB guns.

On the actual day of the anniversary, we all gathered at Grandma and Grandpa's for an open house, everyone dressed in his or her best. All of us boys had to wear jackets and ties and were under strict orders to be on our best behavior. For once, we complied.

I say "for once" because of the phenomenon that usually occurs when boys—of any age—get together in large groups: they become morons. You can see this for yourself in the stands of any professional football game, of course, but I am thinking of the kidhood, McKenzie version of the phenomenon.

We all knew, as individuals, that you could not jump off the chicken house roof using an umbrella for a parachute. Collectively, however, was another matter. Collectively we couldn't wait to try it.

Our parents knew this about us, and so most times that we cousins got together it was under the watchful eye of the McKenzie Mothers' Spanking Cooperative, which worked like this:

Any time we were caught doing something we shouldn't (see above: chicken house, roof, jumping, with umbrella), whatever mother saw us would sound the alarm. The rest of them would drop whatever they were doing—sewing, cooking, cleaning house, talking—and scramble like fighter pilots to the flight line in a World War II movie.

They would run to the scene of the transgression and, working like a team of border collies, begin herding the kids into a little, shrieking knot.

While this was happening, any mother was free to spank any child—her own child, a niece or nephew, some poor kid who just wandered in to see what the commotion was about. Then they began sorting the kids ("Here, Lois, here's one of yours; Mary, you've got two of mine there…") after which we all got spanked again.

Well, on the day of the Very Important That We Behave Fiftieth Wedding Anniversary, we knew any transgression would be answered not only by the McKenzie Mothers' Spanking Cooperative, but the Fathers' Punishment Consortium as well, and whatever we got would be twice as severe as usual, on account of it being a BIG DAY when WE KIDS HAD BEEN WARNED to be on our BEST behavior.

So we were. We spent all day running around in our hot wool

jackets and clip-on ties, saying things like "How very nice to see you, Eldon" and "You're looking well, Grant," instead of our usual conversational gambits: "What's that hanging out of your nose?" and "Bet you can't hit the rain gauge with a BB from twenty feet."

There was a beginning at the anniversary. My cousin, Sharon Kay, brought her new husband, Ken. It was the first time he had ever seen the entire family all at once, and from what I gather it made a profound impression.

That afternoon, after the big party was over, my mother and some of her sisters went over to Aunt Nelta's to fix a little supper for those who had stayed. They whipped up enough beef and noodles to feed one-hundred-and-twenty people. Actually, they made more, but one-hundred-and-twenty is the number that Ken counted lining up for supper. He thought it was staggering. We thought it was normal.

So these are my beginnings: born in Peru, raised in Indianapolis and Washington, D.C., before settling into rural life in LaGrange County, Indiana. One of four kids, one of fifty first cousins. Part of an old and well-regarded LaGrange County family. Son of a farm-boy-turned-newspaperman, son of a farm-girl-turned-newspaperman's-wife, and according to my brother, an occasional son of something else. It is from these beginnings that everything in my life has come, including the stories I tell.

Let's begin.

·⁓ Love Stinks. ⁓·

*In which I establish a pattern that has stayed with me all my
life—shopping at the last minute for a holiday that serves only
to remind me that I do not understand women . . .*

February is my least-favorite month, frozen hands down. For starters,
February in Indiana—especially northern Indiana—is a month of
sub-zero temperatures and head-high snowdrifts. The wind comes
whistling relentlessly out of the north at about seventy miles an hour,
and what little sunlight you get is usually muted by a heavy veil of low,
gray clouds. It is in February that people in LaGrange County wonder
why their forefathers, setting out from Vermont and New York back
during the early days of Westward Expansion, couldn't have made a
left turn somewhere and settled someplace warm, such as Tahiti.

February also has lousy holidays. Groundhog Day? What's that?
We wait around for some rodent to poke his head out of the ground in
Pennsylvania, and from that we are supposed to derive the weather fore-
cast for the near future? Granted, it's generally as accurate as anything
you're likely to hear on the television news, but it still seems like a flimsy
excuse for a holiday in my book. Then again, my book says any holiday
is second-tier if it does not include presents, food or firecrackers.

In February we have President's Day. This is a made-up holiday
if I ever saw one. When I was a kid we at least had two holidays that
made some sense—Lincoln's Birthday on February 12 and Washington's Birthday on February 22. Then some genius in the government decided they should be comglomerated into one holiday which
falls neither on the 12th nor the 22nd, but on a Monday so that workers can have a three-day weekend. Which workers? Government

workers. The rest of us are on the job as usual.

Lincoln's and Washington's birthdays were marked in school by three things: we made silhouettes of Lincoln and Washington in art class; we wrote essays on Lincoln and Washington in civics class; and for lunch on those days we got the little vanilla ice-cream squares with the designs inside—an ax for Abraham Lincoln, the rail-splitter, and an ax for George Washington, who couldn't tell a lie about chopping down a cherry tree. I guess the school systems got a good price on vanilla ice cream squares with little axes inside.

And then there's Valentine's Day. It was a lousy holiday when I was a kid, and it only seems to have gotten worse with time.

Valentine's Day at school DID have the ice cream novelty thing going for it, and this time the ice cream had a heart in the middle of it instead of an ax. But that was about all the good I ever got from it.

It all goes back to the second grade.

I am in Miss McDonald's class and things are going pretty well. I have the reading thing down. I'm doing all right with arithmetic. Really, the work is just a review of the first grade, and I aced the first grade, so second is causing me no real problems so far.

It's February, and we have just finished hearing about Abraham Lincoln, one of the two presidential visages that watch over us from atop the blackboard. The other, of course, is George Washington. Washington I know from the occasional dollar bill that has come my way on birthdays. Lincoln I know is on the $5 bill, but I only know that because my older sister Vicky gets $5 bills to my singles, and likes to wave them in my face before tossing them into her purse and slamming it shut.

So there I am, thinking about lunch (Mom packed me a cheese sandwich that day) when Miss McDonald claps her hands and says she has an announcement.

"Boys and girls," she trills. "Today we have an art project."

Oh, great, I think. *I am behind the 8-ball already.* I was hopeless at art projects. I never could color inside the lines. I always used so much paste that it squished out from behind the paper. And I was simply not to be trusted with glitter. Janitors left nasty notes on my desk after I had to create something involving glitter.

Well, what's it going to be this time? I wonder. *Posters for the library? Papier mache animals? Pencil cups made of soup cans and construction paper?*

"We are going to make mailboxes for our Valentine's Day party next week."

With that, she goes to a closet and hauls out thirty shoe boxes. We file to the front of the room, collect our boxes, a few sheets of red paper and a few sheets of white, and troop back to our desks.

"I want each of you to cover your mailbox with white paper and write your name on the front of it. Then we're going to decorate them with hearts that we'll cut from the red paper."

I am sunk. This is another disaster waiting to happen. Covering the mailbox with white paper is like wrapping a Christmas present, and I already have a reputation in my family as the worst present-wrapper in four generations. Everyone else can turn out nice, neat packages with crisp edges and sharp folds. Presents wrapped by me, on the other hand, look like they have already been opened.

Then there is the matter of the hearts. Other kids—especially the girls—have no trouble folding the paper and maneuvering their scissors so that when they are done, they get perfect little heart shapes. No matter how carefully I do the same thing I never wind up with a perfect heart shape. My hearts always look more like livers.

Once we get the mailboxes done, and the class finishes laughing at mine, with the paste oozing out from behind all those red livers, I put Valentine's Day out of my mind. *I'll deal with it when it gets here next week,* I think. Another mistake.

All the other kids, you see, are smart enough to go out and buy their valentines while the selection is good. Not me. I am one of those kids who waits until a half-hour before the drugstore closes on Feb. 13 to run up to his mom and say, "Mom! I have to get some valentines for school tomorrow!" I had the same attitude about cookies when it was my turn to bring them. Also science fair projects, parental permission slips and homework.

Sure enough, on February 13, we pile into the family Dodge, Mom grumbling, for the drive to the pharmacy. All the way there I get Mom Speech No. 1434, titled "I Don't Know How I Could Have Raised Such Irresponsible Kids." It is not what you would call Happy Motoring™.

We enter the store and head for the aisle that just two or three days ago had been stacked to the rafters with all sorts of Valentine's Day junk—cards, candies, balloons, decorations. Now the shelves stand bare, or nearly so—a few bags of candy hearts here, a few boxes of valentines nobody wanted over there. Glumly, I paw through the merchandise—Wizard of Oz valentines (*The Tin Man says, "Oil be happy if you'll be mine"*), Mighty Mouse valentines (*Here I come ... to wish You a Happy Valentine's Day*) and Teddy Bear valentines (*I can bear-ly wait for you to be my valentine*). The choice is dismal.

After a long fifteen minutes of wishing the stockboy would come bursting out of the back room with a fresh supply of really cool valentines, I give up and decide to go with Mighty Mouse. They seem the least embarrassing.

And then we head for home so I can address them. This can't happen, however, unless I first find the list of classmates my teacher had sent home with me a week earlier. I had filed this where I usually filed school papers: parts unknown.

I look under the bed. There's lots of interesting stuff there—baseballs, toy cars, a few books, a shoe—but no class list. I look in the junk drawer in the kitchen. No class list there, just keys and pens that don't work. I look in my sister's diary (You never know where things might turn up; besides, it's fascinating reading.)

After a couple hours I come to the conclusion that my class list is Well and Truly Lost. This means I will have to address the valentines by memory, which is not the most reliable method of compiling a mailing list. You are guaranteed to forget at least one classmate. More than one, if you are me.

Comes Valentine's Day and off to school I go, toting my freshly addressed valentines in a paper sack. It rains. Not a gentle spring rain, but a cold, relentless February rain. The sack soaks through and the valentines get soggy. The envelopes open and the names, inscribed with penmanship that was none too good to begin with, start to blur. *Terrific,* I think. *What else can go wrong?* It is then that I discover I have forgotten my lunch money.

Now, a cagey teacher would have the kids distribute their valentines in the morning, as soon as they got settled into the classroom. That way you get the excitement—well, for some kids, anyway—out of the way immediately. By noon things will have settled down and you will have a reasonable chance of actually getting some knowledge into their little elementary-school noggins before the 3 o'clock bell.

Not Miss McDonald. She waits until the last part of the day to have the Valentine's Day party, which guarantees that the kids who like Valentine's Day—girls, mostly—think of nothing else the entire day. My mind, too, is occupied, but by dread. You'd be full of dread too if you knew that at the end of the day you were going to pass out soggy Mighty Mouse valentines with blurry writing on the envelopes.

The teacher selects one boy and one girl to be postmen. The jobs, as usual, go to Smirky Judy Gernrich, who tattles on people, and Smug Bobby Foster, who always does projects for extra credit. You know. The brown-noser types, the ones who always throw up their hands at the end of the day to shout, "Miss McDonald! You forgot to give us our homework!" They are, perhaps, the most hated kids in the entire second grade.

Smirky Judy and Smug Bobby come to our desks to collect the valentines. I hand over my soggy little collection, dreading what I know will come next: one or even both of them, staring at the illegible writing, and turning to announce, in a voice that could be heard not only in our classroom but all the way down to the school cafeteria:

"MISS MCDONALD! I CAN'T READ MIKE REDMOND'S SLOPPY HANDWRITING!"

Slowly, I shuffle to the front of the room, to Miss McDonald's desk, to decode the names (Me: "I think that could be Roger Kirby." Miss McDonald: "Who is Roger Kirby?" Me: "Well, then, maybe it's

Elizabeth Robinson.") while my classmates snicker and open their valentines and eat their ice cream squares with the little hearts inside.

Eventually I get back to my desk, spoon up what I can of my melted ice cream, and finally get around to looking inside my liver-festooned mailbox to see what Smirky Judy and Smug Bobby have deposited in there.

The girls, as expected, have given cards with dolls on them (*Barbie says have a Happy Valentine's Day!*) while the boys have concentrated on sports (*Valentine, you're a Home Run!*) And there are one or two Mighty Mouse cards in there, too. It's nice to know I wasn't the only last-minute shopper in the room.

And there is one valentine from a girl who has a crush on me. It is bigger than the rest, with hearts (not livers) drawn on the envelope. And when I open it I see it is one of those off-the-rack valentines, not part of a lot of fify, but an actual, individual card chosen especially for me and inscribed as follows:

"To a sweat boy."

I hope she means sweet.

❋ ❋ ❋

Now that I think of it, though, it could have been sweat.

There is an element of sweat associated with Valentine's Day, of course, but that comes much later in life, when you are an adult. No, not that. Shame on you for what you are thinking.

I am talking about the perspiration of anxiety produced by an adult male shopping for a valentine for the woman in his life: wife, girlfriend, significant other or, as has turned out to be the case in most of my relationships, future ex.

In the years since I have become a so-called adult, I have seen Valentine's Day transformed from what it used to be—Date Night, maybe with candy and flowers thrown in—to a full-blown Second Christmas, and woe to the guy who doesn't rack up some serious Valentine's Day debt on his already-reeling-from-December credit cards.

The thing is, no matter what he buys, he's going to be wrong.

A card? It better be one of the good ones, foil-embossed, or maybe with dried flowers glued to the outside. Whatever it is, it absolutely must come from a quaint little gift shop ten miles out of his way. Under no circumstances should he show up with something he picked up at the drugstore, or worse, the gas station.

Same goes for candy. It must be the deluxe assortment of imported goodies from a little Belgian chocolatier whose work was written up in the Arts and Leisure section of *The New York Times*. Again, absolutely nothing from the drugstore. And no matter how much he spends, the guy should be prepared to hear, "Candy? I can't eat candy! I'm trying to lose weight for Gloria's wedding and you bought me candy?" Nevertheless, he dare not show up at the door without it.

Flowers? Again, the more a guy spends, the happier his life will be. Don't even THINK of buying roses from one of those guys who sits in a lawn chair, next to a pickup truck, in a vacant lot near an intersection. A woman can tell lawn-chair roses at seventy-five feet. And don't try that old "I wanted to get you one, single, perfect red rose" maneuver. To a guy, that says "sensitive" but to a woman it just screams "cheapskate."

Perfume? Forget it. I bought perfume for a girl once. It smelled great in the department store. She liked it, too, until she dabbed it on her wrist and discovered that the interaction between the perfume and her skin created a scent that was not woodsy and musky with a light floral note, as advertised. It was the unmistakable odor of cat pee.

Dinner? By all means, a guy should take his girl to dinner on Valentine's Day. Here, at least, the rules are easy to remember because there's only one: no drive-through.

This gets us to the most dangerous Valentine's Day presents of all: lingerie and jewelry.

Men and women are generally of two different minds where lingerie is concerned. What men think is not printable. What women think of men who think it is also not printable. Let's just say that many a Valentine's Day has been ruined when a woman opens up a package and sees inside what looks like two lengths of ribbon, three tiny lace doilies and a Lone Ranger mask.

Jewelry, of course, is serious business. To a woman, a man who buys jewelry at Valentine's Day is sending one of two signals:

1. I would like to be married, or
2. I have done something awful.

Guys should be careful with jewelry, then. A guy may think he is just buying something pretty that she can wear on her wrist, neck, ears or, if he is a real daredevil, finger. But a woman who opens up a jewelry box on Valentine's Day thinks that someone's life—his—is about to change, radically. She is usually right.

And the second he realizes what she's thinking is when the REAL perspiraton begins.

You can see, then, why I am no fan of Valentine's Day. It's just too sweaty. And that's what I mean when I say love stinks.

·~ Fun and/or Games. ~·

O brother where art thou? Probably getting picked on by me,
that's where my brother art. I mean wert . . .

My brother P.D. is my best friend. This was not always the case.
When we were growing up, he wasn't my friend as much as he
was my victim. My favorite victim.

Now, this wasn't because of any particular malevolence on my
part, or any particular meekness on his. In fact, P.D. was, and is, a
scrapper. There is no one I would rather have on my side in any kind
of fight.

In fact, I wouldn't want you to think that P.D. and I have never
not loved each other. Nothing could be further from the truth.

I wasn't quite three years old when P.D. made his appearance, but
soon I was aware of a change in the family dynamic. The children had
previously been referred to as "Vicky and Mike." Now it was "Vicky
and The Boys." We weren't "Mike and P.D." We were "The Boys."

This made us a team. Mom and Dad further reinforced the no-
tion by dressing us alike from time to time. I can recall one shirt in
particular. It was slate blue with a patch on the pocket. Inside the
patch were two embroidered monkeys. They became known, naturally, as the Monkey Shirts. Rather fitting as insignia go.

P.D. and I shared a bedroom all through our kidhood. We had
circus posters on the walls, model cars on our dresser and toys scattered everywhere; many of them the sorts of things that needed two
participants for maximum fun—slot cars, electric trains, Rock 'Em
Sock 'Em Robots. Remember those? It was a little boxing ring, and

inside were two robots manipulated by hand controls. Press one button, your robot threw a left. Press the other, he threw a right. Tag the other robot on the chin and his head flew off. We loved it. And I can tell you from experience that Rock 'Em Sock 'Em Robots are dreadfully dull if you don't have someone to play them with, like a brother.

We shared more than a room and toys. We shared interests: cowboys, monster movies, comic books, *The Three Stooges*. The only true disagreements, really, came on Saturday mornings when P.D. wanted to watch *Lancelot Link, Secret Chimp* and I wanted to watch *The Beatles* cartoons. P.D. for some weird reason thought that chimpanzees in people clothes was about the funniest thing on the planet. I, on the other hand, was planning to be a Beatle when I grew up, and considered the cartoons to be career research.

So you can see that for the most part, P.D. and I got along fine.

But back then we were subject to the Laws of Nature that apply only to boys in the same family, which is: Big Brothers Pick on Little Brothers.

That's just the way it is.

My age was my advantage. Being two years and several months older, and three grades ahead of P.D. in school, meant that P.D. believed I knew more than he did, not only in arithmetic and science, but in every facet of human endeavor. This was the tool I exploited shamelessly throughout our kidhood.

Sometimes it was just too easy.

It is 1967 and for his tenth birthday my brother has received a new BB gun, a fancy Crosman. I am envious to say the least. A Crosman is a pump model. The front stock is actually the handle to an air compressor, and as you swing it away from the barrel and back again, you pump air into the chamber. The more pumps you give it, the more air you compress and the greater velocity the BB will have upon being fired.

My BB gun is a Daisy Red Ryder model. Dad bought it from the police department in Peru, Indiana when he was a newspaperman there. Some hoodlum was shooting streetlights with it, or so I was told.

I never believed that story because my Daisy Red Ryder is the most anemic BB gun I have ever seen. I'll cock it with the lever and fire and maybe, just maybe, the BB will travel as far as twelve feet, if I have the wind at my back. And on the rare occasion when I do actually hit what I am aiming at, a tin can, let's say, the BB tends to strike the object and fall to the ground without leaving so much as a dent in the can. Any kid shooting out street lights with that gun, I figure, would have to shinny up the pole and blast them point-blank.

So on his birthday I come across my brother shooting cans with his fancy Crosman. The BBs strike the target with a satisfying plink and even knock it off the fence post a time or two. In other words, he is having entirely too much BB gun fun, in my opinion.

So I walk up to him and hold out a hand. "Let me see that gun," I demand. He hands it over and I pump some air into the chamber.

"Take off running," I say, "and I'll hit you in the wallet."

Now, granted, this is a mean thing for me to do. I admit it. But my brother could very easily say "No" and demand that I give him back his gun, and that would have been the end of it. Instead, the Laws of Nature have him in a particularly firm grip that day, because all he does is say "OK" and takes off in the direction of the barn.

Now, I am generally a good marksman. I'm not as good as my cousin, Nate, who can shoot the dot out of the "i" on a can of cream of broccoli soup from one-hundred feet, but I generally hit where I am aiming. And in all due modesty, my shot that morning was spectacular.

As P.D. rounds the corner of the barn, I raise the gun to my cheek and squeeze the trigger. Less than a second later, the BB strikes him right in the—well, not in the wallet, but in the pocket on the other, unprotected side of his buttockular area.

"Hey!" he yells, fanning his hinder and running around the yard. "You missed! You weren't even close to my wallet! Geez Louise, are YOU a lousy shot."

See what I mean? Gullible.

❖ ❖ ❖

Now, just because my brother is gullible doesn't mean that things always turn out as I expect. Take the Case of the Poison Sawdust, for example.

We are living in Bethesda, Maryland. Our house is a half-block from Bethesda-Chevy Chase High School, BCC for short, where Vicky goes to school. At the time, it was said to be the largest high school in the country—a seven-building campus with what were, to us, huge athletic fields.

After school and on weekends, P.D. and I like to go down to the practice field, squeeze through a hole under the chain-link fence, and play. We'll throw a football around, or play catch, or sometimes just romp in the sawdust pits used by the high-jumpers and pole-vaulters. They're perfect places to play Big Time Wrestling. You can lift your brother over your head and toss him to the ground, knowing his fall will be cushioned by the soft, yielding sawdust, and both of you will come up laughing.

That was, in fact, what we were doing one spring evening, just short of suppertime. I have just thown P.D. into the pit, and dived in after him. We're throwing great handsful of sawdust at each other and laughing our heads off when suddenly I am seized by a wicked, Big Brotherly impulse.

I still don't know where it came from, or why. I just know that it was ordained by the Laws of Nature that I must do what I did next.

I quickly affect a somber mood.

"Oh, no," I say.

"What?" says P.D., still laughing and throwing sawdust into the air.

I raise a hand of sawdust to my nose and sniff it, tentatively at first, and then with a little authority.

"Oh, NO!" I cry.

"What" says P.D., his hand frozen in mid-toss.

I let a few tears well up in my eyes and let my voice get choked up.

"Oh, no," I say again, quietly this time.

"WHAT?"

"This . . . this . . . this is . . . the Poison Sawdust."

"Huh?"

"The Poison Sawdust. They put it in here to keep raccoons away."

(Apparently, P.D. does not stop to consider that there haven't been raccoons in our neighborhood of Bethesda, Maryland in something like a hundred years.)

"It looks like regular sawdust to me," says P.D.

"That's how it works," I explain, in my best older-brother-who-knows-more-than-you manner. "The raccoons come in and they don't realize it's poison sawdust. It gets on them and starts working and they don't even know it. They go home and die in their sleep. There's no antidote. And now we have it on us."

I begin to see the first signs of panic in my brother's face. His lower lip trembles. Tears roll down his cheeks. His life is flashing before his eyes and at his age, that's not much of a flash—a few Christmases, a few birthday parties, one or two exceptionally good root beer floats and that's about it. And then he begins to cry—not the soft, snuffling cry I expect, but the deep, mournful wail of someone who had truly lost all hope.

This is more than I bargained for. I just wanted to scare him a little but he is genuinely frightened, terrified even. I am just about to tell him it's all a joke when he jumps up from the pit and runs for home, wailing all the way.

Uh-oh.

I jump up and run after him, but he's moving too fast—panic will do that for you—and has too much of a head start. Just as I turn into the front yard, he crashes through the door, wailing. I hear the words "Mike" and "poison sawdust."

Next thing I know, Mom is crashing through the door in the other direction looking for me. "Michael James Redmond!" she shouts. And with that I know my goose was well and truly cooked.

My mother practices the time-honored Mother Name Code to let me know how much trouble I am in. If she says, "Mike!" it means that she is peeved. "Michael!" means she is annoyed. "Michael James!" means angry—I hear "Michael James!" when I bring home my report cards.

But the use of all three of my names—"Michael James

Redmond!"—means that my mother is furious and that I am once again In For It. And so, head down, I trudge to the house to meet my fate. I'm sad at the punishment I am about to receive, sorry that I scared my little brother so much, but at the same time marveling at just what a pigeon the little twerp can be sometimes.

❖ ❖ ❖

I understand they had spaghetti for supper that night.

I wouldn't know. I was upstairs in my room with a red-hot bottom and the words of Mom Speech No. 732, "I Can't Believe You Would Do Such A Thing . . . Do You Want Your Brother To Grow Up With A Complex . . . Wait Until Your Father Gets Home . . . Maybe What You Need Is A Few Years Of Military School" ringing in my ears.

All because the Laws of Nature made me the older brother, and made P.D. the gullible one.

Not that P.D. was completely without culpability. Not everything that happened to him in kidhood was my fault. Some things he just brought on himself.

When we lived on Brookside Parkway, our first house in Indianapolis, Mom's brother Verl used to like to come visit. He was going to school at Indiana University then, just down the road in Bloomington, and on weekends he knew he could count on square meals and a comfortable bed (usually mine, which meant I got to sleep on the sofa, which I thought was a grand adventure).

We liked having Uncle Verl around. He was fun. Well, most of the time.

The price Uncle Verl had to pay for good food and a comfortable bed was to do things with us kids, such as take us to the movies.

And so it was one Saturday afternoon when Mom tells us to clean up because Uncle Verl is taking us to the theater to see the new Walt Disney film, *Toby Tyler.*

We pile into the car. Vicky sits in front, on the passenger side. I take my customary place in the back, behind the driver. P.D. sits behind Vicky. And because it is a warm day, the windows are rolled down.

We're all excited. We love movies. But P.D. is the most excited of all, and all the way to the theater, for blocks and blocks and blocks, he hangs his head out the open window and yells:

"We're goin' to the movies! We're goin' to the movies."

He yells it to pedestrians. He yells it to kids playing in their yards. He yells it to dogs. And when another car pulls up next to us, he yells it to them, too.

Vicky is embarrassed. I am amused. And Uncle Verl is . . . well, let's just say that was the last time Uncle Verl took us to the movies.

※ ※ ※

Now, sometimes P.D. and I got along fine and played well together. We loved to play catch—especially a game we called "Burnout," in which the object is to throw the baseball harder and harder at each other until one of us chickens out or gets his hand broken. We played a lot of two-man football. Really, about the only time we didn't have fun with sports was in winter.

My brother was born with the basketball gene. He's tall and lanky, ambidexterous, and able to jump fairly high for a white guy.

I had none of these qualities. I wasn't tall, tended to be rather square in shape, was a dedicated right-hander, and had enough leaping ability to touch the top of the doorway, and that was it.

Not only that, I didn't particularly enjoy playing basketball. I liked to watch it, but playing it was another matter entirely. I simply did not have the ability. I had one shot—a two-handed set shot from what seemed like a long way away but, in retrospect, was shorter than a three-pointer in today's game. I could score with some regularity using that shot.

P.D., on the other hand, had an impressive array of skills. He could dribble, pass, fake and, in his high school years, dunk the ball.

Every time we played one-on-one, the game soon deteriorated into P.D. running circles around me and scoring pretty much at will, while I stood out in No-Man's-Land heaving the ball at its distant target. P.D. could beat me severely at basketball. Consequently, I didn't often agree to play him.

My winter game was hockey. I first fell in love with it while reading a book I bought from the Scholastic Book Service, the folks who sold us paperbacks at school. The book was *Captain of the Ice,* about a French-Canadian kid, a wonderful hockey player, who moves to a new school in the U.S. and has to prove his merit against the school's arrogant star player. I thought it was the greatest thing I had ever read.

I began pestering my parents for skates and was one of the lucky kids who found them comfortable from the start. Other kids went clumping around the ice with their ankles turning this way and that, but skating came easily to me, and in a very short time I taught myself stops and turns and cross-overs, and then how to skate backwards, all on our pond up in LaGrange County.

P.D., too, took naturally to skates. In fact, he could skate backwards before I could. And so I guess it was inevitable that we would start playing hockey.

Mom took us to the hardware store, which had a sporting goods department, and we picked out our sticks. I went for a straight-blade model such as I had seen my hero, Gordie Howe, posing with on a hockey card. And then I told Mom she should get P.D. a goalie stick because he wasn't as good a skater as I, which was, of course, a lie. But I had a plan.

We went home and started to play. P.D. had to stand between two overshoes while I blasted him with slap shots. It was fun, but it got boring after a while.

Hockey, after all, was a game of speed and contact. Hockey was bodies hurtling down the ice at breakneck speed, crashing into each other and knocking each other down. Firing frozen rubber discs at your cowering brother had merit, but I craved more action.

And so I induced P.D. to come out of goal and challenge me. He skated toward me. I skated toward him. He braced. I slammed into him with all the force I could muster, turned a hip sharply, and pitched him right into a snowbank.

"Let's do it again," I said.

And the fool got up and skated back toward me.

Again he went into the snowbank.

This, I thought to myself, *is what I call fun.*

P.D. had other thoughts. As he lay in the snowbank for something like the twentieth time, he unlaced his skates, looked up at me and said, "Hockey is just another excuse for you to beat me up."

I hated it when he was right, but what could I do? It was the Laws of Nature.

Which ended, by the way, when P.D. was sixteen, nearly as tall as me and a much better athlete. We were goofing around with those old boxing gloves—the ones I wore for a picture when I got a black eye—and he caught me with a left, square on the end of my nose. I saw stars. I had to sit down. It became apparent in a flash that the Laws of Nature had changed, and no longer would I be able to treat my younger brother as anything but an equal. For the first time in my life, for the first time in any contest with my brother, I said, "I give."

And we've been best friends ever since.

The P.D. I know as an adult is a bright and talented guy, well-read and insightful, who has the quickest wit of anyone I know. People tell me I'm funny, but if you want to be reduced to helpless laughter by an endless stream of rapid-fire asides and one-liners, P.D.'s your man.

A guy has two kinds of brothers: those he was born with, and those he chooses. In the latter category I list a special few: Frank Dean, Tommy Healy and Steve Greenberg. These are the guys with whom I share a bond so deep as to be inexplicable. I know that if I were to call them at three in the morning to say "I'm in trouble," their first response wouldn't be "What's wrong?" It would be "I'll be right there."

P.D. has the distinction of fitting into both categories. If he hadn't been born my brother, I would have chosen him.

~ Dad. ~

*Early Dad, Late Dad, Almost–Too-Late Dad—I lived with
them all, and it was weird. Fun, but wierd . . .*

My sister Amy tells me I sound just like Dad on the phone. I can live
with that. My brother P.D. looks like Dad—we're talking the image of the old man, from the beetling brows to the mustache—and he
has to face it, so to speak, every time he looks in the mirror. Nothing
bugs him more than people calling him "Pat"—that's what Dad went
by, so my brother is "Patrick" outside the family—and then adding,
"and you look just like your father!" Believe me, he knows it.

I guess you could say that P.D. and I, like a lot of guys, have had
our Dad Issues. They don't get much buzz anymore, but a few years
ago Dad Issues were big news. Remember that Iron John movement
or whatever it was called? It was some sort of male-empowerment
thing with guys running off to the woods together on weekends to
beat on drums and pretend to be Indians and mostly to talk about how
their fathers were distant, and how they never measured up in their
fathers' eyes. Then it sort of died. I guess the guys finally figured out
that their fathers were, by nature, distant and demanding. It was just
the way their generation behaved and there's not a whole lot we can do
about it. We're all in the same boat, the *SS Sons of Distant and Demanding Fathers*, so there's no sense complaining about it. So much
for Iron John.

P.D. and I have long divided our life with Dad into three distinct
eras: Early Dad, Late Dad and Almost–Too-Late Dad.

Early Dad was the dad of our kidhood, and a great Dad he was.

He wasn't an imposing man—five-foot-ten, one-hundred-sixty pounds—but he had presence. Black hair, dark brown eyes, olive skin, and a bristling black mustache on his lip during a time when mustaches were not in vogue. Clark Gable, Adolph Menjou and Dad wore mustaches, and that was it as far as I could see.

He was quiet and dark and, I guess, kind of scary and mysterious to the other kids in the neighborhood. Of course, we couldn't see that. He was just Dad to us. To them, though, he was thousands of miles removed from what their concept of what a dad should be.

For one thing, he worked at the newspaper. All other dads in our neighborhoods seemed to work in factories where people made things, like car parts or telephones, except for Jim Mellene, two doors up the street. He was a deputy sheriff.

For another, he worked weird hours. He was on the state desk of an afternoon newspaper with early deadlines, so he was gone from the house well before sunrise every morning, and home in the middle of the afternoon. The other dads, as I recall, were more of the eight-to-five variety except, of course, for Mr. Mellene.

And he wasn't one of those suburban buddy-boy types, even though we lived in the suburbs then and buddy-boy was the order of the day. He tended to keep to himself—didn't spend a lot of time popping brewskis and watching the ballgame with the neighbor guys.

For all these reasons, the other kids all thought we had a weird dad. To us, they couldn't have been further from the truth.

What we had was a fun dad, especially where cars were concerned. For some reason, cars brought out the joker in Dad.

Take, for example, the time he went downtown to pick up our new 1962 Pontiac Tempest convertible from the dealer. This was Dad's baby, a car he had dreamed about getting, so it was a huge day. And with him he took P.D., who was five.

Dad settled up with the dealership, put down the top, installed P.D. in the passenger's seat and began to cruise back toward the far eastside, where we lived. He was on a four-lane street—two going east, two going west—when he hit a stoplight. He braked the Pontiac to a halt in the inside eastbound lane. A car with a large man driving pulled up beside him in the outside lane.

My brother, who had been quiet up to this point, noticed the car next to him. He turned his head, looked the driver in the eye and said, "If you can't drive it, park it, !@?*head."

Dad died a thousand deaths behind the steering wheel right then. It might have been a thousand-and-one, but the light changed and he was able to pull away before the other guy could get out of his car.

If he was angry at P.D., he didn't show it. It wouldn't have made sense, anyway. He knew where P.D. learned what he said. Nobody else in the family talked like that. And when he got home we all went for a ride: Mom driving, Vicky in the front passenger seat and P.D., Dad and me perched on top of the back seat, waving to the neighbors as we paraded around the block. It was Dad's idea.

Family legend says I once saved Dad from a ticket. This was before we got the Pontiac. We were in our caramel-and-crème 1957 Dodge Coronet, I believe. Anyway, Dad ran a stop sign and got pulled over by a police officer.

He read Dad the riot act while Mom sat embarrassed in the passenger seat and we kids watched in amazement from the back. Dad was known for having a sharp tongue and a quick temper and there he was, sitting silently while Officer Friendly chewed him out.

I was sitting directly behind Dad. The officer saw me back there and turned toward me. I guess he saw that I was more or less awestruck. I was in my law-and-order phase at the time, influenced no doubt by a steady diet of Roy Rogers TV shows in which the good guys always triumphed, the bad guys paid the price, and the man with the badge was the undisputed best good guy of all. The lines were clear to me: good was what you wanted to be and bad was . . . well, bad.

So Officer Friendly turned to me and said, "Well, what should I do with him?"

"Put him in jail," I answered.

Dad got a warning.

This was Early Dad: a dad who loved cartoons as much as we

did; a dad who made chicken on the grill, basted with garlic and butter, on Sunday afternoons in the summer; a dad who sat down with us kids to draw pictures for a half-hour before supper.

Early Dad used his big, black copy pencils from work to draw tattoos on our arms, and watches on our wrists. He played the ukulele (quite well, in fact) and sang. He took us to the movies. He took us skiing in Michigan and swimming in Florida.

Early Dad played catch with us, watched cartoons with us, and tucked us into bed with bristly mustache kisses. Early Dad was wonderful.

One thing we got from Early Dad that stays with P.D. and me is an unreasonable love of firecrackers. Dad was, to put it mildly, a firecracker nut. For him, the highlight of our one and only family vacation to Florida was driving back through Tennessee, where they had all those roadside fireworks stores with the goofy names: Crazy Charley's, Loco Joe's, Nervous Norman's. We visited them all, and we stocked up. We came home from Florida with enough ammunition for the next three Fourths of July.

In later years, we went to Ohio for our firecrackers. There was a curious law in place at the time that allowed Ohio merchants to sell firecrackers to people who were not from Ohio. There was another law in place at the time that made it illegal for Indiana residents to bring into the state firecrackers from Ohio.

Therefore, the annual Early July Firecracker Expedition was planned, and carried out, with all the precision of an international smuggling ring.

"Wake up." I hear my father's voice calling gently from the door to the bedroom. "We're going to Ohio."

It takes us a second to realize what he has said. Ohio? Who do we know in Ohio? Ohio? Then, at last, it hits us. We're going to Ohio! Firecrackers.

P.D. and I jump out of bed, pull on our clothes, and run downstairs. Dad is in the kitchen, drinking coffee and smoking a Newport. P.D. and I wolf down a couple of bowls of cereal, rush through our chores and in twenty minutes are out the door and heading for our white Ford convertible.

The weather is warm, so Dad puts the top down. This is the way we like to travel: just us guys, the open road and nothing over our heads but sky—dark sky at the moment, but we can see the sun throwing a few streaks of orange onto the eastern horizon. It will be light by the time we get to Ohio.

Instead of taking the Toll Road, which would get us over the state line in less than an hour, Dad steers east on a two-lane state highway. We go past farms where people are still finishing their morning chores. We can see lights burning in the milking parlors, and up at the houses, in the kitchens. We glide through small towns just getting a start on the day: a guy in an apron standing in front of a restaurant, smoking a cigarette, a woman wearing a headscarf getting into her car.

What we do not see are cops. This is Dad's plan. Leave under the cover of darkness and stay off the big roads so we don't run into police officers looking to crack down on firecracker smugglers.

The sun is fully up when we roll past the sign that reads "Entering Ohio." Instantly, the condition of the road changes. The tarmac is smoother, without the gnawed edges we know from the roads in Indiana. We know this because Dad tends to drive way out toward the edge of the highway, and whoever is in the passenger seat—me, in this case—tends to take a beating, bouncing up and down through that crumbling pavement. For the way my Dad drives, Ohio is a nice, comfortable state.

We see a fireworks stand, the first one across the state line from Indiana. Dad zooms by. "Too obvious," he says. Same with the second, and third and fourth. It seems like we are going to go clear to Toledo before Dad finds a place he can be sure is not under the watchful surveillance of the Indiana Undercover Cherry Bomb Cops.

Finally, he whips the car off the road and into a dusty lot under a banner that says "Fireworks!" We pile out and, following Dad's lead, walk coolly to the stand. Dad does the shopping—an armful of Black Cat firecrackers, all lined up nice and neat in the red-tissue wrapping. A box of M-80 cherry bombs. A double fistful of bottle rockets. A half-dozen Roman candles.

Dad settles up and we head for home with the booty stashed under the rear seat of the car. "Never put them in the trunk," Dad says "That's the first place they look."

We boys are instructed to sit in the back and, if we get stopped by a cop, to keep our mouths shut. I guess Dad is concerned that if a police officer pulls us over, one of us—perhaps the one who once told a cop to put him in jail—will spill the beans. Either that, or his other son will try to help by saying something like, "Don't look under the rear seat for firecrackers or anything." Which, now that I think about it, is precisely the sort of thing P.D. would have done.

And home we go, by a different state highway, staying well within the speed limit (not easy for Dad) and moving carefully through the traffic (also not easy; he tended to be rather a daring passer and lane-changer).

Not once are we stopped by a cop. In later years, P.D. and I discussed the matter and decided that the reason for that was because we never even SAW a cop on our fireworks-smuggling expeditions. Ever. It's not like they had roadblocks set up at the state line looking for Pat Redmond, International Fireworks Smuggler. The cops, it seems likely, knew good and well that any car with Indiana plates heading back from Ohio in early July probably had firecrackers in it. They just had other, more important work to do.

As we pull into our drive, though, Dad credits his clean getaway to careful planning and execution. We believe him. We have just come back from Ohio with illegal fireworks, and we are thrilled out of our skulls. He is our hero.

❊ ❊ ❊

That was Early Dad.

Late Dad was a different guy altogether.

Late Dad is our way of saying "Mid-Life Crisis Dad." We didn't know, back then, what it was called. We just thought he was goofy.

He did the whole Who Am I, Where Am I Going, What Have I Done With My Life bit, and it was, to say the least, difficult. He got a girlfriend, left Mom, lost his job with the congressman, took a job editing *The LaGrange Standard*, grew his hair long and cultivated a beard to go with it (for a while there, I called him the Willie Nelson of journalism, although I made sure to do it behind his back), and bought a sports car. Well, HE thought it was a sports car. It was an Opel GT. I guess it might have been a sports car if he ever could have gotten it running.

I was in my late teens and early twenties then, and Dad and I grew far apart emotionally. I hated what he had done to Mom, hated what he had allowed himself to become, but was too intimidated by his frequent rages to do anything about it. I simply disappeared for long stretches of time.

My brother, however, was right in the thick of it, and he fought with Dad every single day. Every day, that is, until Dad came bursting into his room and rousted him out of bed, rudely, and P.D. had simply had enough. Before he knew what he was doing he was up and out of bed, grabbing Dad by the shirt front, lifting him up and pushing him to the wall. Dad was pinned there, his feet dangling a good six inches off the floor.

This was when my brother realized he had not fully thought out his plan of action. He did not know what to do next.

Gently, P.D. let Dad slide to the floor.

"Don't do that," he said.

Dad left the room without a word. I think P.D. shut the door and collapsed with relief.

Now, I don't want you to think the Late Dad days were without any sort of fun. It was there. It just wasn't like it used to be. I think that was the nature of the conflict for us boys. Early Dad we absolutely loved. We loved Late Dad—he was our father, after all—but we didn't like him.

We did laugh at him, though. For instance, when he made chili. Dad was a serious chili aficionado, as am I, as is P.D., and he was proud of the chili he made. It was good chili, but what I liked best about it was watching Dad cook. It was pure theater: hours and hours of chopping and mincing, slicing and dicing, stirring and tasting, that left the kitchen in a wreck. And the way he carried on about it, so seriously and earnestly, you would have thought he was brewing up Top Secret Longevity Potions. Or Rocket Fuel. Actually, recalling the taste of his chili, Rocket Fuel is more appropriate.

Dad always liked hot chili. At the time, what other Hoosiers passed for chili was a watery hamburger-tomato-kidney bean soup, usually with elbow macaroni floating in it, so Dad considered his chili—thick, meaty and hot as blazes—the Real Deal, and himself a Culinary Trendsetter.

However, as Dad got older, his taste buds seemed to go haywire. Maybe it was all those martinis he drank, or all the cigarettes he smoked. Maybe it was all the chili he had eaten. Anyway, the older Dad got, the hotter his chili became until, toward the end, it was just plain inedible. We did find, however, that if we scattered it around the perimeter of the yard, we were never bothered by owls.

❊ ❊ ❊

That was Late Dad. Almost-Too-Late Dad refers to Dad in the last year before he died. His kidneys had failed some years earlier, requiring him to take three trips a week to South Bend, fifty miles away, for dialysis. For quite a while he had kept up some semblance of a normal life—well, normal for him, anyway—but now the rest of his body was following the lead of his renal system. Dad was dying.

One of the first things he did in that last year was ask to move back home and Mom, God bless her, took him in. She says it was because it was the decent thing to do, but I think she's lying. He was the love of her life. She could have refused him if she wanted to, but she didn't want to. He needed her, and I think in a way she needed him, too, as sick as he was.

Sometimes during that year, Mom says, she and Dad would talk the night away like they had done as newlyweds. He was clear-headed and peaceful and, I think, sorry for the wreckage he had caused in the turmoil of his middle years.

I can't say we grew close then. Frankly, I loved my father but I still didn't trust him, but with Mom's help I came to understand how much he loved me and how proud he was of what I had done with my life. The distance between us closed somewhat, and for the first time in my life I felt that I did, in fact, measure up.

I had gone into the newspaper business not from a great desire to be a reporter, or because I liked to write, although those feelings were present, to be sure. But the real reason I became a newspaperman, I now realize, was to get my father's approval. I knew in my rational self that he approved of me all along, but my emotional self believed otherwise. Maybe, it reasoned, if I followed him into journalism, I would get that approval I so wanted. And in that last year of his life, I did.

Then Too-Late Dad was upon us. As his body grew weaker, his mind began moving in new orbits. One afternoon I spent an hour with him at the Publix Café in Kendallville. Well, that's where HE thought we were, anyway. In fact, we were in a hospital room in South Bend. He also thought it was 1946 and that I was a fellow named John Kaiser, and that there was a Benny Goodman record on the jukebox.

Dad died in April, two weeks shy of his sixtieth birthday. I was a music critic then at *The Indianapolis News*, and I was covering a concert by John Hiatt. I came home to find the message on my answering machine: my mother telling me to call immediately. I called. It was too late. Dad was gone.

It was two o'clock in the morning. I went to the office and wrote my concert review. Then I wrote Dad's obituary, and started the long drive to LaGrange County.

We buried him in Brighton Chapel Cemetery, right on the south edge of town. I drive past it every time I go home to visit Mom. You can see his tombstone from the road: "REDMOND." I always honk on the way to Mom's, and I always stop to visit on the way back. When the visit is over, I look for a stone to place atop his marker, the

way Jewish folks do at their cemeteries. Not only do I like the tradition, I like knowing that the cemetery caretaker must be wondering
why in the world someone keeps putting rocks on Pat Redmond's
headstone.

And the only Dad issue I have now is that I miss him.

·~ Mom. ~·

I want a girl just like the girl who married
dear old Dad. Or do I?

It's a tricky thing, a guy's relationship with his mother. Make too
much of it and they call you a mama's boy, or worse. And for those of
you who don't know what I mean, let's just say that Oedipal Complex is
not the name of a new apartment community on the west side of town.

A guy's relationship with his mother is deep and complicated,
moreso even than his relationship with his father. A dad and son can
share a deep and abiding love and never show it, unless, of course,
their team wins the Super Bowl, at which point they are likely to jump
into each other's arms and, in the more exteme cases, kiss each other
on the cheek—but even the toughest of us can be turned into a mass
of quivering Jell-O by his mother.

I can recall one such example from my days as a reporter covering
criminal courts. A bigtime drug dealer was on the stand, singing his
head off in hopes of a reduced sentence. Without much direction from
the prosecutor, he was giving names, dates and places that would lead
to some serious jail time for at least six other bad guys.

Then his mother walked in. Instantly the guy's demeanor changed
into something none of us—the prosecutor, the judge, the cops, the
reporters—had ever seen in him. Before his arrest, he was cocky to the
point of arrogance. On the stand, he was contrite. But when his mother
walked in, he just dissolved. This big, tough, long-haired, bearded,
tattooed, gun-toting man turned into a whimpering three-year-old.

Of course, I should probably mention that his mother was one of the six bad guys he was ratting out. That might have had something to do with it.

Although we never went into the freelance pharmaceuticals business, my relationship with my own mother is no less complicated than that guy's. She has been my friend, my confidante, my greatest source of strength. She has also been a nag, a scold, and nothing short of unreasonable (especially during my teenage years; back then I thought all adults were unreasonable).

But what my mother has been, mostly, is remarkable.

At one point in her life she was raising four kids at four distinct and dramatic points in their lives: a senior in college, a senior in high school, a ninth grader, and a kindergartener. And she did it alone. Without killing any of us. Remarkable.

Mom changed through the years, of course. It wasn't as drastic as the Early Dad/Late Dad/Almost Too Late Dad continuum, but even so the Mom of my kidhood and the Mom of my adulthood are vastly different.

Mom today is a kind and loving woman who religiously follows Indiana University basketball, would eat fried potatoes every meal if she could, and who is given to passing along advice to her sons, such as "Happiness is a decision you make. Decide to be happy, and you will."

Kidhood Mom was loving and kind, to be sure, but she ran the house with an attitude best described as no-nonsense. Which was smart. Thanks to my brother and me, there was plenty of nonsense already present.

I seem to recall her always in the kitchen in those days, and always doing something that shortened her temper, sometimes to hilarious, although unintended, effect.

It's summer, about 1963 or so, in a suburban neighborhood on the east side of Indianapolis. I'm outside with the neighbor kids—Lanny from next door, Jeff from across the street, Tim from two doors down. We've just completed a rousing game of cowboys and are wondering what to do next.

For some reason—I can't remember why—the talk turns to

mothers. Mine, according to the consensus, is the strictest on the block. The consensus is correct. Mom does not let us play outside after dark, like Lanny's mom lets him. Mom insists that I practice the trombone an hour a day, usually while Tim and Jeff are outside playing. Mom won't even let me ride my bicycle in the street. I have to stay on the sidewalk until I am twelve—that meant three more years, an eternity in Kid Time—while Lanny, Jeff and Tim are free to go whizzing up and down Gilmore Road.

"Your mom's mean," says Lanny.

"Yep," I agree.

"She never lets you do anything fun," he adds.

"Yep."

"And she has a big nose."

Now this one I had not thought about.

It's true that my mother has a sharp nose. It's the McKenzie nose, passed down through the generations going all the way back to which-ever McKenzie it was who wandered down from the highlands of Scot-land to come to America and start our branch of the family. Grandpa McKenzie has it, Mom has it, all twelve of Mom's brothers and sisters have it. It never seemed particularly big to me. It just seemed like the Family Nose.

Not that any of this reasoning pops into my head when Lanny says Mom has a big nose. I just say, "She does not."

Lanny, no slouch in a debate, answers with lightning speed.

"She does too."

"Does not."

"Does too."

"Doesn't."

"Does."

And with that, I am stymied.

I jump up and run into the house to ask Mom what to do.

I burst through the back door into the kitchen, where Mom is up to her elbows in something—canning pickles, I think. She has her back to me.

I breathlessly recount the events of the Great Side Yard Debate, the details spilling from me in a torrent of "he saids" and "I saids." Mom appears to be listening thoughtfully. At least, that's what I think. What she's really doing is standing there with her back to me, concentrating on the pickles.

"So what should I do, Mom? Huh? Huh?"

Without turning around she says, "Oh, just tell Lanny to go to hell."

This is stunning.

Hell, as you know, is a Bad Word. I am not allowed to say Bad Words. Only adults can say Bad Words. Such as my father. He says Bad Words all the time. Mom says it is because he is a newspaperman, and newspapermen are notorious for their liberal use of Bad Words.

But now I am standing in the kitchen and I have just been given maternal permission to use a Bad Word. Me, a nine-year-old, given permission to cuss. This was better than being allowed to ride my bicycle in the street. I couldn't have been happier if Mom had tossed me the car keys, handed me a wad of $100 bills and pointed me in the direction of the toy store.

"OK," I chirp. "Thanks, Mom!"

I run back outside to the side yard. By this time, the other guys have disappeared—off to ride their bikes in the street, I imagine—but I figure they're still within earshot, so I take a deep breath, cup my hands around my mouth and yell:

"HEY, LANNY! MY MOM SAID TO TELL YOU TO GO TO HELL!"

And then the strangest thing happens. The neighborhood falls silent. Lawnmowers stop running. Birds stop singing in the trees. Dogs stop barking.

No doors slam. No car engines roar to life. Fathers stand motionless at their barbecue grills. Mothers pose like statues behind their screen doors. Two girls playing jump-rope are frozen in mid-leap. All you can hear is my voice, echoing down the block: "Hell-hell-hell-hell." Time has come to a halt and it is all because of me, Swearing Boy.

I'm standing there, admiring my new-found powers, when I feel a hand gripping my shoulder and spinning me around. It is my mother.

"What did you say?"

"I said what you told me to say."

At that moment, Lanny's mother comes to life and bursts through her screen door. She walks directly up to my mother and begins reading her the riot act: *Your son has a filthy mouth* and *What kind of mother are you* and *We never use that kind of language in our house.* That last one, by the way, was an out-and-out falsehood. Lanny himself taught my brother P.D. the dirtiest joke in history, which P.D. repeated at the dinner table one night, which caused my father to turn all red in the face and Mom to gasp in horror. Vicky and I laughed and we had to finish our dinners in the kitchen.

Mom stands there as Lanny's mother continues her rant. Mom's face gets darker and darker. Her hand clutches tighter around a wooden spoon she carried out from the kitchen—to spank me with, I suppose. My many years of experience in getting on Mom's nerves tell me that she is near the point of explosion, so I back away, gingerly. I am almost to the back door when it happens.

"Yes, I did tell him to say it," she says to Lanny's mom. "What's more, I meant it. Go to hell."

And with that she turns and stalks back into toward the house, sweeping me into the kitchen ahead of her where . . . well, I wish I could say we have milk and cookies and a big laugh over what has just transpired, but we don't. Instead, I get five smacks on the butt with the wooden spoon for using a Bad Word.

For some reason, she does not agree when I point out that she also used a Bad Word and therefore should be subject to five smacks from me. I am given to understand that I am just a kid and it is different for adults. Adults can use Bad Words and ride their bicycles in the street.

❋ ❋ ❋

The Mom I know today is quite a bit changed from the Mom of

my kidhood. Every once in a while this surprises me. I don't know why. I'm certainly not the same person I was forty years ago. Why should I expect her to be the same person she was forty years ago?

Today's Mom lives at the home place north of Brighton with her two indoor cats, Ivan the Terrible and the Princess Anastasia. My mother is fond of giving her cats Russian names. I suppose it is as good a time as any to point out that we're not Russian.

Outside, she has a number of cats living in the garage. I say "a number" because I am never quite sure how many there are, and neither does she. Whenever I go up to visit I see a few new faces among the old familiars running around the yard.

That my mother is fond of cats should be apparent by now. It is, to everyone but her. "I'm not a cat lover," she says. "I'm a cat LIKER. I don't love them, but I like them."

Yes, it was that deep sense of "like" that prompted her to spend hundreds of dollars on surgery when Ivan the Terrible ate half a spool of thread. A deep sense of "like" that moves her to drag home fifty-pound bags of kibble or boil up thirty chicken necks for the outdoor cats. A deep sense of "like" that makes her call on Sunday morning and begin, without even so much as a hello-how-are-you, with an update on the kittens that one of them gave birth to a week ago last Thursday. Yeah, she's a cat liker, all right.

What Mom has done in the last fifteen years or so is reduce her life to the essentials: her cats, her birds (she has several bird feeders hanging on an old swingset, right outside the dining room window, and despite all the feline presence this bird cafeteria gets quite a bit of business). And her basketball.

Oh, is my mother crazy about basketball.

Winter nights find her parked in front of her television set with a game blaring away. Her first preference is for Indiana University basketball. She has been a devoted IU basketball fan since 1950, when Dad was going to school at the Bloomington campus and they were living in the trailer court that was married students' housing at the time. They were poor as churchmice, of course, and basketball games on the radio were their chief source of entertainment.

Mom cried, of course, when the university fired head basketball coach Bob Knight. She was one of that peculiar breed of little old Hoosier ladies known as Bobby's Girls. You would see them every-where—grocery stores, airports and occasionally even a basketball game. They were the ones padding around in their red-and-white sweatsuits with an IU pennant in one hand and a cowbell in the other. Which I admit is a strange getup for a trip to the grocery store.

Bobby's Girls defended their Bobby. It was never Bob Knight to them, always Bobby, with a loyalty that bordered on the absurd. If he had robbed a liquor store, hijacked a bus full of school kids and set fire to a church, they would have found a way to excuse it. "Oh, that's just Bobby," they would say, chuckling. "He's always been kind of high-strung."

Many Bobby's Girls swore off IU basketball when Knight was fired and transferred their loyalties to Texas Tech, the school that hired him. Not Mom. As far as she was concerned, it just made things better. Now she had two teams to root for.

My mother has an Adaptable Scale of Loyalty that allows her to always be interested in a game. It works as follows:

At the top of the heap is IU basketball. That's her favorite team, and if there's an IU game on the air, that's the one she'll watch. After that, in descending order, her preferences are:

Purdue University, any other team in the Big Ten (in the case of a conference game, the team closest geographically to Brighton, Indi-ana is her favorite), any other Indiana college, any other Midwestern college, and, finally, any other college in the United States, including Alaska, Hawaii, Puerto Rico and Guam.

Oh, wait. I forgot Texas Tech. That comes between Purdue and the rest of the Big Ten.

When there is a basketball game on the air—which, thanks to Mom's satellite dish, means "every night between October and March"—Mom will sit there, riveted. She does not like to be dis-turbed. Which is why I try to call her at least once a week when I know she's watching a game. It goes like this:

Ring
"Hello?"
"Hi, Mom. It's me."
Silence.
"Mom?"
"Yes?"
"I was just calling to see what's going on."
"St. John's is leading by two."
"Oh. Well, I kind of had an interesting day at work. This guy came up to me and . . ."
"Oh my God!"
"Mom? Mom? What's wrong?"
"He missed the lay-up."
"Ah. Well, like I was saying . . ."
"Just a minute. Oh, that can't be right. I can't believe this. That isn't what happened at all."
"Huh?"
"Technical."
"Oh, well, like I was saying, Mom, I've decided to have a sex-change operation, rename myself Christine and make my living dancing naked on tabletops in front of strange men."
"That's nice, dear. Can you call back in a while? Thanks."
Click.

You'll notice my mother did not say goodbye before ending the telephone conversation. She's been doing this for the last ten years or so. I think it's genetic because her mother did the same thing. You'd be talking to Grandma on the telephone one second and all of a sudden she'd be done and the line would go dead. No goodbye, no see you later, no nothing. Just a click and no more Grandma.

I once made my grandmother very angry because of the way she talked on the telephone. She called the house at least once a day, and if one of us kids answered ("Redmond residence," we said, never "Hello"; we all considered it quite liberating when we got out of the house and were finally able to answer the phone like regular people) Grandma would invariably ask, "Is your mother handy?"

On this particular day when Grandma called with her usual inquiry, I answered, "Yes, I think she's very useful."

And then I hung up without saying goodbye.

You may rest assured I got into all kinds of trouble for it when Grandma called back and told Mom what I had done.

The quality that comes to mind first when I think of my mother today is serene. She's happy with her life, comfortable with her own company, and keeps as busy as she wants to be, which these days isn't very busy. She lives one day at a time, and enjoys those days as thoroughly as she can.

If you ask her, she will tell you that her greatest accomplishment was raising four children to adulthood without any of us going to prison. It's a guaranteed laugh-getter. I think there's also a kernel of truth to it. For a while there P.D. and I had her a little worried.

But when she tells that joke she sells herself short. From the middle of a pack of thirteen kids, she found a way to be heard and to be herself. She persevered through a marriage that was, at the least, difficult. She prepared thousands of wonderful meals without getting much back in the way of thanks. She endured four dramatic teenagers. She took more than her share of bumps, jolts and falls along the way, but it never changed her loving and giving nature. Mom is still the aunt my cousins call when they need someone to talk to.

My mother decided to be happy, and she is.

Her greatest accomplishment is her own life.

·– Dozens of Cousins. –·

You call it a family reunion. I call it eating fried chicken and green bean casserole with several hundred people, all of whom know way too much about each other . . .

I have among my possessions an eight-by-ten photo taken in 1962 at the farm of Nathan R. and Marion (Troxell) McKenzie. It shows a bunch of people, a big bunch, gathered under a boxelder tree on a summer day. In the background is a bunch of great late-Fifties and early-Sixties cars—two-tone Plymouths with big rear fins, an old rusting pickup truck. Our blue 1962 Pontiac Tempest is nosed in over by the grain bins.

This is a photo of the entire McKenzie family as it existed in 1962.

At the center, in lawn chairs, are Grandma and Grandpa. They are holding my Aunt Margaret's twin babies, Linda and Laura. Next to them is Grandpa's dog, Hoss.

And arrayed all around them are their children and grandchildren. The adults, including Mom, and the big kids, including my sister Vicky, stand in rows behind them. The little kids—including my brother P.D. and I—stretch out in the foreground, a long line of little blond children seated in the grass and squinting at the camera.

The person you do not see in the photo is my dad, because he was the photographer. This photo ran eight columns across in *The Indianapolis News* along with a story, written by Dad, with the headline:

Dozens of Cousins Swell the Count at Family Reunion.

Dozens of cousins. That's my family.

Mom was the ninth of the children born to Nathan R. and Marion (Troxell) McKenzie. They had seven girls and six boys, and if that wasn't enough they took in one of Mom's cousins, too, to make a grand total of fourteen children who called them Mom and Dad.

When my generation came along, our parents did as they were taught by example and had a lot of kids. I am one of fifty who knew the aforementioned Mr. and Mrs. McKenzie as "Grandma and Grandpa."

Looking at it now, it seems huge: I have fifty first cousins on my mother's side. That is a staggering number of first cousins. I didn't think so when I was a kid, though. I thought it was normal. And people who didn't have fifty cousins, classmates that had six or seven, let's say, seemed underprivileged to me.

We seemed to be born in clusters, bursts of natal activity every few years that served to divide us into distinct groups. There were the older cousins, who were already adults by the time I came along; the big kids, the group that included my sister Vicky, four years older than me; my gang, which all the cousins, boys and girls, born within two years either way of my birthdate; the little kids, which was my brother P.D.'s group; and the babies, which included my sister Amy. Amy, born in 1966, is the youngest of all the McKenzie cousins.

I can honestly say that I liked, and still like, all of my cousins, but there are a few for whom I have special affection. John Swihart, for example, the son of Aunt Nelta and Uncle Maurice. We're about the same age, and we were very best friends when we were little guys. If our families both happened to be at Grandma and Grandpa's the same day, John and I would run off together looking for some trouble to get into. We usually found it.

The chicken coop, for instance. We found lots of trouble there. Well, actually, we found lots of eggs there, and that's what led to the trouble.

It's a hot summer day in 1960 and Johnny and I are looking for something to do. We've already explored the barn. We've poked around the garage. We took a walk up the lane to the woods and back again. And now we find ourselves in the chicken coop.

John reaches under a hen and coaxes an egg out of the nest. I do the same. It's warm and smooth and it seems heavy, somehow. We stand there, bouncing the eggs in our hand, when suddenly we are seized by a devilish impulse: to find out what they sound like when you throw them against the wall.

Which we then do.

Incidentally, I can tell you that an egg thrown against the wall makes a very satisfying "splat." So satisfying, in fact, that we go back to the nests for more ammunition.

This is actually a big deal. There are hens on those nests, and they don't particularly care for us, and express this by pecking our hands and arms. For us to keep diving in past those beaks, we really have to enjoy throwing those eggs.

A few minutes later, we stop. We've splattered about two dozen eggs all over the inside of the chicken coop. There are more eggs in the nests but we don't want to get carried away, so we fly the coop, so to speak, and move on to other adventures. And, just to show what morons we are, we don't even attempt to clean up after ourselves. It never even crosses our minds. We just leave the eggs, with their shards of shells and broken yolks, right where we put them on the walls. I guess we think nobody is going to notice.

Well, someone does: Grandpa.

Now, this is where it gets interesting for me.

I am just as guilty as John. I certainly smashed as many eggs, maybe more. And I had enjoyed myself. But John is the one who gets in trouble.

I receive a relatively light sentence—a spanking from my mother, which to tell the truth is not really as big a deal as I make it out to be with all the howling and crying. It's just a spanking, after all. I've been through it hundreds of times.

John, however, feels the full weight of the McKenzie Family Justice System. By that, I mean that in addition to receiving several parentally administered swats to his hiney region, he also had to deal with the fact that Grandpa is mad at him. In our family, having Grandpa mad at you is like being excommunicated. You are cut off. An outcast.

Branded. And it is awful, just awful. Being out of Grandpa's favor hurts far worse than any spanking.

The reason Grandpa is mad at John and not me is because John lives on a farm and I do not. At this time, we live in Indianapolis. According to Grandpa's reasoning, John should have known better than to throw eggs at the chicken coop walls. I, on the other hand, being a city kid, was not expected to understand that this was wrong.

Of course, Grandpa is in error. I know full well that I was in the wrong, and I was every bit as responsible as John. But I am not about to correct my grandfather. No way.

So I let John take the heat.

I've always felt a little bad about that, but not bad enough that I felt like I should apologize to John or anything. Besides, he got me back several times over in later years. We're even.

⌗ ⌗ ⌗

My cousin Nate, one of Uncle John and Aunt Mary's sons, was my boyhood hero. I idolized Nate and wanted to be just like him when I was eight and he was fifteen. Nate, I was pretty sure, was the coolest person in the world. Of course, you have to remember that my world wasn't all that big back then.

Nate liked to hunt and fish. I liked to fish and although I hadn't done much hunting, I liked the idea of it. It involved guns, and I was in my G.I. Joe-Roy Rogers phase. I had every toy gun made, a regular kid arsenal right there in my toybox, and was anxiously awaiting the day I could grow up and shoot the Real Thing, like Nate.

Nate also knew about girls, or at least said he did. This was important. They weren't high on my list at that particular moment, but I knew I was going to need the information someday.

Nate and his sister Laura spent a few weeks with us the summer between my sixth and seventh grade years, when we lived in Bethesda, Maryland. Uncle John and Aunt Mary thought the trip would be educational. It was, but not in the ways they expected.

Next door to us lived the Harrisons, who had two teenage daughters—Barbara, a statuesque brunette, and Francie, a willowy blond with long straight hair. It is my adult mind that uses the words "statuesque" and "willowy." Back then I didn't care all that much. They were girls, and older girls at that, and I was uninterested in statuesque and willowy.

Nate, on the other hand, was completely interested. And never was his interest keener than when the Harrison girls would put on their bikinis and lie in the sun in their back yard, which as luck would have it could be seen, in its entirety, from P.D.'s and my bedroom window . . ..

"Be quiet," says my cousin Nate, holding a finger to his lips as he tiptoes across the bedroom to the window overlooking the Harrisons' back yard. "You don't want to spook 'em. You'll need to know this when you get older and we go hunting." I presume he means for squirrels. Turns out Nate has other game in mind.

It is one of those blistering hot days that are the norm for summer in the Washington, D.C. area. The air is thick and humid. Dogs lie panting in the shade. The only humans who dare to venture out are the Harrison girls next door, who sunbathe daily in their back yard in their bikinis.

This is what Nate is hunting. He caught a glimpse of them when he arrived a week ago, and every day since then he has parked himself by the window, not in it, where he might have been seen, but off to one side, so that if the girls happened to look up that way, they would see only a window with its curtains fluttering.

P.D. and I sit with him while Nate comments, in a whisper, on the qualities of the girls.

"Francie looks like a lot of other girls," he informs us. "She's slender and has that straight blond hair. Every other girl looks like that these days. But Barbara"—her brunette older sister—"now Barbara, she's got sex appeal."

P.D. and I have not a clue as to what he means. We can only judge from Nate's enthusiasm that sex appeal is a good thing for a girl to have.

I am content to watch and learn, but P.D., always the more impatient brother, thinks someone ought to take some action. He's tired of sitting next to the window watching Nate watch the girls. The thing to do, he decides, is to introduce Barbara to Nate.

So he pops his head into the window and yells:

"Hey, Barbara! My cousin Nate thinks you're pretty!"

I don't know how Barbara reacts. I am too busy watching Nate as he flees from the room, his face turning seven different shades of red, to spend the rest of the afternoon reading magazines in the basement.

❊ ❊ ❊

As I got a little older, my bubbling-over intense hero-worship of Nate settled into a simmer. We moved to LaGrange County, Nate went off to college, and the gang of cousins near my own age became my running buddies. There was John Swihart, of course, but also Grant (Nate's brother, a year older than me), Eldon Keith and Scott (Uncle Eldon and Aunt Betty's boys), Greg (Uncle Bruce's son who died tragically in a work accident a few years later), and, on occasion, Grant's sister Mary Beth, who was my age. John, Grant, Mary Beth and I all went to school together at Brighton. The other guys lived out-of-town—Eldon and Scott in Indianapolis, Greg in Lafayette—so we only saw them on weekends or in the summer.

Eldon and I had been exceptionally close when we lived in Indianapolis. What I liked about Eldon was the fact that something exciting always happened when he was around, thanks to his inability to resist temptation. Eldon was a bright kid, a good kid, but he had one character flaw: whenever he came up to the Behavioral Boundary Line, the one that marked the difference between Being Good, as we usually were, and Being Stupid, it brought out the devil in him. He couldn't resist taking one giant step into Stupid Land.

For example, the time he found a dud firecracker in the yard. He tossed it casually into the charcoal grill, where it detonated, just as Mom was about to start cooking hamburgers.

Or the time he took my Red Ryder BB gun, which Mom kept by the back door to discourage a certain stray dog that had taken to using our backyard as a bathroom. Eldon picked it up, pointed it at me and shot me right in the hip. I wasn't hurt, but I played it for all it was worth, anyway: "I've been shot! Eldon shot me! Am I bleeding?"

And Eldon uttered the cliché of all clichés, which also happened to be the truth: "I didn't know it was loaded."

Eldon was disciplined by his father. That happened a lot. In fact, "Eldon's getting a beating" became a sort of rallying cry for the rest of us cousins. We'd be scattered around the yard at Grandpa and Grandma's, just hanging out, when Scott or Eldon's other brother, John, would send out the word: "Eldon's gettin' a beating!" And we would all gather near the house to find out why or, if the information was not available, speculate on what Eldon had done this time.

When I entered eighth grade at Brighton, John and Grant took me under their wings, showed me around, introduced me to their friends, did whatever they could to make the transition easier. Frankly, I needed it. A year before I had been part of a class of several hundred seventh-graders at Leland Junior High in Bethesda. Now I was one of twenty-two eighth graders at Brighton, a fish out of water in the worst way.

I have only been in this school three days, and I'm still very much on my guard. I have the basics down: I can find my desk in the big room that all the classes use as home room. I'm pretty sure I know where the restrooms are. I'm beginning to put some names with some of the strange faces Grant and John have introduced to me.

Eighth and ninth grade boys take Physical Education together at Brighton School. Not only does it help with scheduling, but combining the classes is the only way we can get enough boys together for a decent game of . . . well, anything. These were small classes.

In Physical Education class, I tend to hang back. I haven't yet had my adolescent growth spurt, and I feel like a shrimp compared to the big, strong farm boys who surround me, and so I keep to myself, quiet, trying to figure out how I might start playing with these gorillas without getting trampled.

We've just finished a game of dodge ball. My team—captained by my cousin Grant—has just beaten the other team, captained by his classmate Danny Rinkel, although not by any special effort on my part. I did my best to get hit and thus out of the game quickly, the better to observe from the sidelines.

Now I am in the locker room, getting out of my gym clothes, when out of the blue Danny Rinkel decides to take my measure. Looking back, I don't blame him. I was the new kid. Danny was just establishing his turf.

"Hey, squirt," he says. "Anyone ever tell you what a runt you are?"

And he smacks me on the shoulder.

"Huh?" I answer. Even at that young age, I was the master of the snappy comeback.

"You heard me, runt," he says, and smacks me again.

Now I'm mad.

"I'm sorry," I say. "I wasn't paying attention. I was too busy looking at your upper lip. Are you trying to grow a mustache, or did you have chocolate milk for lunch?"

Evidently I stepped on a nerve. Danny was proud—unduly so, if you ask me—of the cookie duster he was cultivating on his upper lip, even though it really wasn't much more than a few wispy strands of peach fuzz. Despite his pride, Danny must have known deep down inside how truly pathetic it was, because he comes after me like I had just scored a direct hit on his ego, both fists flying.

Danny is about a foot taller than I, and a good thirty pounds heavier, and so I am, to put it bluntly, getting the crap knocked out of me. And this is what Grant sees when he comes through the door to the locker room.

"God damn it, Rinkel!" he cries, and the next thing I knew, Danny Rinkel is upside-down in the showers with Grant standing over him, glowering, his fists clenched.

"Leave my cousin alone," he says.

I never had trouble with Danny Rinkel again. In fact, we got to be friends.

❀ ❀ ❀

Grant also introduced me to one of the great loves of my life. No, it wasn't a beautiful woman. If it had been a beautiful woman, Grant would have kept her for himself. Family loyalty has its limits, you know.

No, it was through Grant that I was introduced to motorcycles.

All of us McKenzie cousins have the motorcycle bug, to one degree or another. For this you may credit our Uncle Verl, Mom's youngest brother, who rode an Indian motorcycle in the 1950s, when we were at our most impressionable.

Grant still talks about his first motorcycle ride, on the back of Uncle Verl's Indian. "I remember looking down," he says, "seeing the pavement going by, beneath my feet, and thinking *This is cool.*" Grant knew at that moment that he was going to be a motorcycle rider.

I took the ride on Uncle Verl's bike that same afternoon and, frankly, I was scared half to death. I couldn't admit that to Grant, though, so when I climbed off and the next cousin climbed on—Uncle Verl gave a LOT of rides that afternoon—and Grant asked how I liked it, I said it was cool, too. Grant beamed with cousinly approval. The more we talked about it, the less scary it became to me. Before long, Grant and I were pestering Uncle Verl for second rides, and thirds.

That was it. The die had been cast. At that moment it was clear that we were going to be motorcycle guys, which is exactly how it turned out. Grant at this writing has a half-dozen or so in the garage on his place up in LaGrange County. I have one sitting in my garage. When we get together at the family reunion each summer, we always seem to pair off and talk about motorcycles. Then Eldon joins us, and John. Soon we are joining up with other cousins—the older ones and the younger ones, the boys and the girls. The older we get, the smaller are the differences between us, and the greater the bond we share.

One thing we have in common is growing up with the feeling that we didn't measure up to the standards set by the McKenzies. McKenzies have a strong streak of perfectionism, and with it an absolute conviction that their way to do things is the right way to do them.

After spending most of my adolescence trying to disprove the latter, I finally gave up a few years ago and admitted to myself that they were right. Not that I told them.

A few years back I built raised tomato beds in my backyard. That night, I had a dream in which I was visited by all my McKenzie uncles, who were inspecting my tomato beds and shaking their heads. Uncle Van said it didn't look like I had used pressure-treated lumber. Uncle John said I hadn't adequately prepared the soil. Uncle Eldon thought the corners were sloppy. Uncle Bruce saw that the posts were out of line. Uncle Dean said I had planted the wrong varieties of tomato for the climatic zone I'm in. And Uncle Verl just laughed and said he doubted the boxes would last a week and I'd be lucky if I got one edible tomato out of the patch.

The next day I went out, tore up the boxes, and rebuilt them again to McKenzie standards.

A few months later, at the family reunion, a number of my cousins came up to me, one at a time, and each one whispered the same thing to me:

"I've had dreams just like that one you had about the tomato boxes."

The heart of our cousin-ness, of course, is our shared memory of Grandpa and Grandma. Without exception, every single one of us counts Nathan and Marion McKenzie as among the greatest people we have ever known. The generation after mine is full of little boys named Nathan. We don't have as many Marions as we should, but we have a lot of little Nathans.

What strikes me about our family reunion talk is how each of us had a unique relationship with our grandparents. In a brood the size of ours, you'd think a few kids would feel as if they were lost in the shuffle. Nope. Every single kid has special memories of a time when Grandpa and Grandma gave them the special attention every kid wants, and needs, and deserves.

My own favorite goes back to when I was about five.

There are bunches of us kids up at the farm that day, but I've wandered away from the crowd to watch Grandpa cultivating corn in the field north of the house. I stand in the orchard, leaning against a gnarled old apple tree, and watch him make pass after pass, the cultivator shovels digging carefully between the rows of young, green corn.

Grandpa finishes up in time for lunch and pulls into the orchard. "Get on," he says. I run over and grab his outstretched hand and he boosts me onto the seat of the big, green Oliver 77 tractor. He pulls down the throttle lever, lets out the clutch and we chug back out into the field to make one more pass.

All the time Grandpa is explaining to me how the cultivator shovels dig out the nutrient-stealing weeds from between the rows of corn, which will result in a better crop in the fall. Most of it goes over my head. Besides, I'm so excited at being on an Actual Moving Tractor that I can't concentrate on much more than how wonderful it is. Still, I feel like Grandpa is imparting some Very Special Knowledge to me, and know that I must be very big indeed for my Grandpa to take me into his confidence like this.

He pulls out of the field and stops in the orchard. "Go on up to the house," he says. "And don't tell the other kids I gave you a ride, or I'll have to give tractor rides all day."

I keep quiet almost until I get to the back porch, where I see a half-dozen or so of my cousins milling around. And then I just can't contain myself any longer.

"HEY YOU GUYS!" I yell. "Grandpa gave me a ride on the tractor!"

And yes, he does spend much of the rest of the day hauling grandkids around.

❖ ❖ ❖

These are the sorts of things we talk about at the reunion. We talk about what a great kidhood we had, being part of a big, rambunctious Indiana family. We talk about being McKenzies. We talk about Grandpa and Grandma.

We talk about how wonderful it is to be cousins.

⋅∽ Sarge. ∽⋅

There are patriots, and there are Patriots, and then there was
the man who brought fireworks to Mongo, Indiana . . .

Of the holidays that do not involve receiving presents or eating large
meals, my favorite is the Fourth of July. I suppose I get some of it
from my father, who was crazy about the Fourth of July and told wonderful stories about his own kidhood, getting up early and setting off
firecrackers all day long—little ladyfingers to greet the day, strings of
Black Cats at noon time, booming cherry bombs as night fell.

But I think I also have my own, personal love of the day that
comes, pure and uninfluenced, from somewhere deep inside myself.

It is in summer, my favorite time of year; it celebrates American
independence, which I value; and it involves fireworks, which I have
loved as long as I can remember.

When I was a little kid, Mom and Dad would take us (Vicky, me
and P.D.—Amy's birth was several years away) to the Butler Bowl in
Indianapolis for the yearly fireworks display. My memories of those
shows are hazy. About all I can recall with certainty is that they had
spectacular ground displays. I seem to remember one in particular that
was a moving teeter-totter with, I believe, a witch on one side and a
bear on the other. Then again, I might have hallucinated it, because
that was the same year that all three of us kids came home from the
fireworks and woke up the next morning with the mumps.

I have seen a lot of fireworks since. I particularly enjoy the ones
they fire off the roof of a building in downtown Indianapolis every
Independence Day. I can see those from my backyard. I've seen good

fireworks displays at theme parks and ball parks and grand openings.

But the best fireworks I ever saw were the ones Sarge Frye brought to Mongo.

Mongo is a little LaGrange County town, about four-hundred or so people, three miles south of our home place. And Wesley E. "Sarge" Frye, owner of the Mongo Tavern, was its greatest character, a man of legend even before he died.

Legend has it that Sarge killed the previous owner of the tavern and claimed as the spoils of victory not only the business, but the man's wife, Loretta.

Legend also has it that Sarge was born Amish and was plowing a field one day in the 1940s as an Army recruiter drove by the farm. Sarge dropped the reins and ran catty-corner across the field to catch up with the recruiter, jumped into the car and went off to enlist.

Legend further has it that Sarge was assigned to the Army Air Corps where he became a gunner and assistant flight engineer on B-25s, that he saw many of his buddies shot out of the sky around him, and that is what turned him into what men called "a heavy drinker." The ladies of the town sniffed and called him a drunk.

Like most legends, it had some basis in truth, especially the last part. Sarge DID like to drink. In addition to being the tavern's owner, he was also its best customer. In fact, some people said Sarge—who in his first job, after the war, had driven a bread truck for a bakery and did his drinking as a customer, like the rest of us—bought the tavern because it was more cost-effective.

The Mongo Tavern was situated in what once had been an old bank building on the main intersection—the "four corners," in the language of northeastern Indiana—in Mongo. After the bank failed during the Depression, it became a barber shop. My mother remembers getting her hair cut there.

Eventually, it became a tavern, although vestiges of its banking past remain. Inside, you can still see where the old vault used to be. Sarge kept a cooler in there.

It wasn't much as bars go—four stools, five or six tables, a jukebox and a coin-operated bowling machine. It served beer and wine only, no mixed drinks. It was dark, intimidating to first timers, but wildly entertaining when Sarge was holding court.

If you wanted to catch Sarge in any sort of lucidity, you had to do it early in the day. At noontime he was relatively clear. By mid-afternoon, he was in a state we might call pleasantly pickled. By evening, he was gassed. This is why, when you wanted to eat one of the ham sandwiches, for which the tavern was justifiably famous, you waited until late afternoon to do it.

A sandwich ordered at lunchtime would be just that: a serving of fried ham in a soft white bun. But a sandwich ordered later in the day, when Sarge's blood-alcohol level was on the rise, was an architectural marvel—a half pound or more of ham, teetering on the bun, topped with a gigantic slice of raw onion and a scoop of dill pickle relish, with a generous lashing of mustard and a dollop of horseradish. People drove for miles to get one of Sarge's late-afternoon sandwiches.

Those who waited until evening, however, were frequently disappointed. By then Sarge was so thoroughly gone that his sandwich-making abilities went into sharp decline. The ham might be burned, or he might forget the onion and horseradish. He might even forget to make the sandwich altogether. No, if you wanted to feast at the Mongo Tavern, your best opportunity always came between 3 PM and 6 PM.

To us kids, Sarge was a character, and a likeable one. Any kid who chanced to be in the general store when he was in there got a candy bar, on Sarge. Without fail. Sometimes we would wait around the corner on our bicycles, watching the front door of the tavern for Sarge to come out and go trundling across the street to the store.

Dad parked alongside the tavern one afternoon and went inside to pick up a six-pack. I was nearly grown, so I went with him, but we left Amy, then six, in the car—a white Ford convertible that happened to have the top down that day.

Dad bought his beer and exchanged pleasantries with Sarge, who looked over his shoulder and saw Amy in the car. He handed Dad two Mounds bars. "For the little girls out there." It seems Sarge had first seen Amy in the front seat and looked away. When he looked again, she had jumped into the back seat. Sarge thought she was a set of twins.

One thing Sarge was exceptionally proud of was his status as a veteran of World War II. He belonged to every American Legion and Veterans of Foreign Wars post in a three-county area. The inside walls of the bar were plastered with patriotic memorabilia; pictures of Sarge's Army buddies and over the jukebox, a sixteen-by-twenty portrait of Franklin Delano Roosevelt, in Sarge's opinion "the greatest by-God president the United States of America had ever known."

Sarge also was a dedicated Democrat, which helped add to his legend in overwhelmingly Republican LaGrange County. Every four years he mounted a campaign for county sheriff. He might have made a run for it had he gone out and actually campaigned, but Sarge preferred to make his speeches across the bar at—not to, but at—whoever happened to be in the tavern at the time. When he got wound up, as he always did around election time, his speeches could go on for hours: long, rambling dissertations about war and peace and government crookedness and draft-dodgers, all of which had not a thing to do with enforcing the law in LaGrange County, Indiana.

Frequently during these speeches, he would come out from behind the bar, lurch across the room to the jukebox, drop in a quarter and punch in the number for Kate Smith singing "God Bless America." This happened at least four or five times a night. Sarge would demand that everyone in the tavern sing along.

It was during this time that Loretta, who then was living with Sarge without benefit of clergy, although they later married in a ceremony right there in the bar, would make her presence known. She would stand in the center of the room and sing along in a voice that could peel paint. Then she herself would drop a quarter and play "If You Got The Hoss, Then I Got The Saddle," which she would perform, complete with dance steps. The Mongo Tavern thereby became the only beer-and-wine-joint in an old bank building in a small town in Indiana that also had a floor show.

One spring in the late 1960s, Sarge was in one of his patriotic rants when he decided that what Mongo needed, by God, was fireworks for the Fourth of July. Wolcottville had fireworks. Topeka had fireworks. Nothing would do but that Mongo have fireworks, too. He grabbed an empty pickled-egg jar from the storeroom, set it on the bar, threw in a five-dollar bill and declared that the Mongo Fourth of July Fireworks Fund was officially accepting donations.

From that moment on, anyone who set foot in the bar was expected to contribute. No, make that required to contribute. Occasionally Sarge would help them decide by putting the change from their purchases directly into the jar for them. Others he simply scowled at until they made a donation. And by these methods, Sarge raised something like fifteen-hundred bucks in a few short weeks.

Back then, you could buy a lot of fireworks for that kind of dough, and Sarge made sure to spend every penny of the dough on the best-quality explosives he could find. He knew that this was going to be his Big Show, and he was determined to make it memorable.

Came the Fourth of July and that evening, people began gathering in the field next to the Methodist Church on the north side of Mongo. Some came to see fireworks, I guess, but it's fair to say most of the people came to see what sort of foolishness that old drunk Sarge Frye had gotten himself into.

But the scoffers were thwarted. Sarge came through, big time.

As the sun dipped below the horizon and the last streaks of day yielded to the soft, summer twilight, Sarge detonated a mortar shell that boomed loud enough to be heard four miles in any direction. He followed it immediately with a volley of bright, flashing chrysanthemums and fountains, splashing red and silver sparks across the sky.

One after another the fireworks soared over our heads—red and green, blue and orange, sharp concussions followed by rattling string pops, like machine-gun fire. Each round of fireworks was more spectacular than the last, until it all culminated in a grand finale that was an orgy of sparks and noise, flashing and booming, with a giant American Flag ground display crackling and sending showers of red, white and blue sparks cascading to the ground.

It was the greatest fireworks display any of us had ever seen.

The next year rolled around and the pickled-egg jar went back onto the bar. This time, we couldn't wait for the fireworks display. Those poor folks in Wolcottville and Topeka didn't know diddly-squat about fireworks, we said. Compared to our Mongo fireworks, they were shooting off bottle rockets and waving sparklers.

And son-of-a-gun if the second year's fireworks weren't better than the first.

To see Sarge at those fireworks displays was to see a man in his glory. He supervised every detail, from the placement of the cannons to the parking of the cars. And when one of the fireworks went sideways instead of up, setting fire to the woods behind the field—a ground display we had not expected, but applauded anyway—Sarge jumped onto the Mongo Volunteer Fire Department's grass buggy and directed the firefighting efforts, too.

By the fourth or fifth year, the Mongo Fireworks had grown into a BIG DEAL, indeed. People came from all over northeastern Indiana to see them, and the show itself turned into an all-day celebration, with ball games and food stands. One year, Jay Gould from The Little Red Barn radio show on WOWO (the big voice of the big business of farming) came up to make a patriotic speech.

It was about this time that some of the more somber, respectable Mongo folks (ladies, mostly) decided that the fireworks had become far too important to be entrusted to that old drunk, Sarge Frye. They organized themselves into a committee, elected officers, formed subcommittees (entertainment, refreshments, crowd control) and told Sarge that the celebration had become just too big for one person and they were doing him the favor of taking over. He could, however, be co-chairman of the fireworks subcommittee, along with the volunteer fire chief, if he wished.

Sarge told them what they could do with their committee. I can't tell you what it was exactly, but I will say that a committee's worth of people would not easily fit into a place so small. And that was the end of his involvement with the fireworks.

They went on that year and frankly, they were pretty good. But without someone like Sarge, who cared about the Fourth of July more than just about anything else in the world, the committee soon began falling apart in the kind of backbiting, sniping way that can only happen in small towns, where every dispute, including those over civic celebrations, is personal. In a few short years, the Mongo Fireworks were history.

But Sarge kept on celebrating. Every Fourth of July he would put up a tent in the yard next to the tavern and host a day-long celebration, with beer and patriotic music and free hot dogs for the kids. It wasn't the fireworks, but it was a pretty fine way to spend the Fourth of July, just the same.

In the field north of the church, right about in the same spot where they used to set off the fireworks, is a cemetery. In the middle of the cemetery is a flagpole, with an American flag fluttering proudly, directly over a grave. Sarge's grave.

It is, I think, a fitting resting place for a legend.

·~ The Golden Age of Kidhood. ~·

*Everybody thinks his or her kidhood was the best time to grow
up, and I'm no exception. The difference is,
I happen to be right . . .*

I *think of August as a golden month*—golden sunshine pouring onto
the fields; long, golden days of leisure; golden sunsets sending us
into the warm night. And it is in August that I feel closest to my kid
self, the one who grew up in the Golden Age of American Kidhood.

I started calling my kidhood by that name a few years ago, when
I first became a columnist and was looking for a smart-aleck way to
introduce a few stories about my growing-up years. I lifted the phrase,
I now admit, from my friend and colleague David Mannweiler, who
for years had used something similar to describe the earliest days of
his newspaper career, when he was a boy working in the company of
men, including two unforgettable characters named Albert and Edwin.

Albert and Edwin were copy boys. They were grown men who,
we would say in a phrase we think is sympathetic but which actually
runs closer to condescension, were "a little slow." Old-timers who once
worked at *The Indianapolis News* can spend hours over drinks telling
wildly entertaining stories about Albert and Edwin, and while the
stories are always cushioned by what can only be called affection for
these men, you also can't help but feel that the stories were told from
the point of the intellectually superior bemused by the actions and
remarks of people whose mental abilities were not at their level. Except for David.

What David realized as a boy in their company—proving, I think, that children intuit things that adults, with all their accumulated layers of fear and doubt cannot—is that people like Albert and Edwin might not be as smart as the rest of us in the widely held sense of the word, but have nonetheless figured out their own way of dealing with the world, methods which we so-called normal people might find amusing, but which work perfectly well for the Alberts and Edwins. That was their genius, and from their point of view, the way they did things made perfect sense, and it was we, not they, who were out of step.

David referred to this time in his life as The Golden Age of Copyboys, and that is what I shamelessly took and adapted to my own purposes when describing my kidhood.

At first it was, as I said, merely a convenient handle for the stories I wanted to tell. But as I looked further into it, I began to realize that it was, indeed, the truth. I did grow up in the Golden Age of American Kidhood—the 1950s and 1960s. I believe there was no better time to be a kid in this country.

We were, in many ways, the center of the universe. Our parents had come through the Great Depression and war and, having paid that price, were eager to live the Good Life: a house, a car (maybe even two!) furniture, appliances, televisions, record players and kids to raise in the midst of all this bounty.

Bounty. That was a big part of the golden age of kidhood. Toymakers, candy companies, comic book publishers were all working second and third shifts to meet our demands; demands created by television networks that set aside huge blocks of programming with which to fill our minds with cartoons and, more importantly, commercials.

We felt like we were the center of the universe, and in many ways, we were. Life for us was a rich parade of candy bars—Milky Ways, Snickers, Three Musketeers, Mounds, Almond Joy, Zagnuts, Clark Bars, Bit-o-Honeys, Wayne Bun Bars (maple, please) and the one candy which was, by neighborhood acclamation, the best of them all: Bonomo Turkish Taffy.

I can still sing the jingle: B-O. N-O. M-O. Bonomo! Oh! Oh! Oh! It's Bonomo (Turkish Taffy).

I don't know what, if anything, made it Turkish. I do know that it was dangerous to your dental work. I ripped out a space maintainer gnawing on a piece of Turkish Taffy—chocolate, I'm pretty sure.

What made it so good was not the candy itself, but the way you ate it. The technique was to slap the taffy—hard—on the sidewalk or step. It was brittle, and this would break it into bite size pieces you could share, if you were so inclined. Most of the time, we were.

The breaking was the important thing. Every day of our lives our parents were on our backs about not breaking things. Don't play ball in the house, you'll break a window. Don't hold your milk like that, you'll drop it and break the glass. Don't turn the TV knob so fast, you'll break it. Get down off that roof, you'll break your neck.

Here was something we were not only SUPPOSED to break, we were ENCOURAGED to break. And it was FUN. You'd wind up and slap the bar flat against the concrete and hear that satisfying CRACK! as the taffy broke into all those pieces. No other candy gave you that kind of fun for your nickel. Mr. Bonomo, wherever you are, I salute you.

There were other candies, too. Gumdrops, the fruit kind. The spice ones were favored by old ladies, such as my grandmothers. Licorice whips. Mary Janes. BB Bats. Kits. Boston Baked Beans. French Burnt Peanuts. Brach's Maple Nut Goodies.

All of which went exceptionally well with Frostie root beer, I might add. It was my preferred drink then, although I did like the occasional Canada Dry ginger ale, and some of the more vivid flavors of Pokagon pop, a northeast Indiana local brand that came in colors so bright you could almost hear them hum. The grapefruit pop was especially good, as I recall, and the grape was so intense you practically staggered at the first sip.

These would be consumed either while reading a comic book (*Superman* for me, *Spiderman* for P.D., although we both shared a deep love for *The Green Lantern*, and we both were known to use *Classics Illustrated* when we had a book report due the next day) or watching television.

On weekday mornings we had *Captain Kangaroo*, with Bunny Rabbit and Mister Moose, followed by *Miss Frances* and *Ding Dong School*. We watched *Romper Room* a few times, but we never got with the program where that do-bee stuff was concerned.

There would be more cartoons at lunchtime, and after school: local shows, and good ones, with lots of the great old *Popeye* cartoons, the one where he mumbles all the time and where the bad guy is Bluto, not Brutus. Brutus came later and he was never as good as Bluto.

We had *Astro Boy* and *Gigantor*, from Japan. All that Japanese animation you see today? It was around forty years ago. We just didn't know it was anything special.

And then came Saturday. Glorious, wonderful Saturday. We'd be up before dawn to make sure the zenith was warmed up. We would park ourselves in front of our sets, in our pajamas, cereal bowls in hand, ready for a broadcast day that began with *The Three Stooges* at 7 AM and ended with a *Bomba the Jungle Boy* movie at 1 PM.

(Actually, in my earliest viewing days, the first thing I watched on Saturday mornings was *Howdy Doody*. P.D. doesn't remember it. *Howdy Doody* went off the air before P.D.'s memory circuits started to work, I guess. Too bad. His loss. It was a great show. I STILL love *Howdy Doody*.)

We watched everybody we could: Rocky and Bullwinkle, Yogi Bear and Huckleberry Hound, Jerry Mahoney, Bozo, Superman, Mighty Mouse, Heckle and Jeckle, Johnny Quest, Space Ghost, My Friend Flicka, Sky King, the Lone Ranger, Deputy Dawg, Mister Magoo, Woody Woodpecker, King Leonardo and, of course, the greatest of them all: Bugs Bunny and Daffy Duck.

Scattered through them all, of course, were the commercials, for peanut butter, for candy, for potato chips and soft drinks, for cereals and especially for toys. We watched them all, and pestered our parents for everything we saw. Especially the toys.

From as far back as I can remember, my brother and I were of two distinct minds where toys were concerned. There were my brother's preferences—toy trucks, toy cars and especially G.I. Joes—and then there was what was right.

By that I mean toy guns. All through my kidhood, I was armed and ready. If a toy company made a gun, chances are I had it in my toybox.

My preference was for anything made by Mattel™. I was a dedicated Mattel man. "You can tell it's Mattel, it's swell" was more than a slogan to me. They were the words by which I lived.

The Mattel toy gun, as I repeatedly lectured the playmates who toted inferior (in my view) Hubleys™ and Marxes™, was the most realistic toy gun on the market. And realism was everything to me.

I was, I admit, a bit of a snob about it, so much that I customarily threw a fit when someone showed up wearing cowboy guns when we were playing Army. They just weren't *right*, I would argue.

My arsenal was good for any contingency. If we were playing Army, I could choose from several models of .45 automatic sidearm, plus a tommy gun or an M-1 carbine, depending on which rank I had been assigned. If I were a sergeant or higher, it was the tommy gun, because that's what Sergeant Chip Saunders carried on *Combat*, one of my thirty-six favorite can't-miss TV shows of the time. If I was a lowly corporal or private, I got out the M-1.

For cowboys, I had an equally large selection but tended to stick with my trusty Mattel Fanner Fifty with genuine cowhide holster. It saw me through range wars, Indian uprisings, holdups, posses and all manner of sagebrush mayhem. Occasionally I carried a Winchester rifle as well, but most of the time I was perfectly content to tame the West with my Fanner Fifty—holster worn on the right side if I was pretending to be Roy Rogers, swung around to the left side; if I was Wild Bill Hickock, practitioner of the deadly cross-draw, the holster was on the left with the butt facing out.

For the times we played cops, I had something no other kid on the block could match: A Mattel (I told you I was dedicated) Dick Tracy Snub-Nose .38 with the snap-draw shoulder holster.

This made a huge difference. With that shoulder holster, I could carry a concealed weapon, which in the kid pecking order qualified me to be a detective. I was the elite. The other guys, with their guns on their hips, had to be beat-pounding flatfeet. I was the brains of the outfit.

Of course, wearing a shoulder holster did present a problem. By nature it had to be concealed. There wasn't much point otherwise. The trouble is, in order to conceal it I had to wear my Good Jacket, the red one with the gold buttons and the little patch over the pocket, and my mother, for some reason, was adamantly against my wearing the Good Jacket with the gold buttons and the patch over the pocket out to play. Therefore, I had to sneak it out of the house when she wasn't looking, and sneak it back in later, and be extra careful not to get it grass-stained.

Off I would go, trotting down the street on my way to shoot it out with a bunch of bank robbers in Tim Mellene's yard. I would be wearing my standard kid uniform: dirty sneakers (U.S. Keds were my brand, except for the year when I inexplicanbly switched to Red Ball Jets), Billy-the-Kid jeans with patches over the holes and worn knees, a T-shirt stained with grass, chocolate, blood and orange Kool-Aid—and over it all, a crimson blazer. Wool. In summer. I must have looked like an absolute moron.

As I said, my brother did not share my love of toy guns, with one notable exception: a Johnny Reb cannon he and I received from Grandma Redmond one Christmas. It was spring-loaded and could fire little plastic cannonballs, about the size of a billiard ball, up to about thirty feet—more, if you raised the elevation by putting a couple of phone books under the wheels and caught a good tailwind.

This clearly elevated our status in the neighborhood. Every kid on the block had toy guns, but the Redmond boys had artillery.

We also had an outside stairwell leading down to the basement of our house, and it came together with the cannon and the Redmond brothers to provide one of the more dramatic afternoons in the Golden Age of Kidhood.

The stairway was protected on two sides by iron railings about three feet high. This made it a perfect submarine or fort, and we used it often for just those things.

Then our mother planted scarlet runner beans at the base of the railings. As they grew in, they provided cover. Now we had a foxhole, a machine gun nest, or—as was the case this afternoon—camouflage for our artillery placement.

We were there to protect the house from the invasion of our back yard by forces so sinister as to threaten our very way of life: our sister, Vicky, who was about twelve at the time.

She was hanging up the laundry. In fact, she had just come out the basement door with a basket of wet sheets and towels and a bag full of clothespins. P.D. and I were standing there in the stairwell. "Get out of the way, morons," she said as she pushed past us. Which, if you look at it the way we did, made what happened next Her Own Fault.

We swung the cannon into position, poked the barrel through the excellent cover provided by the scarlet runner beans, and took aim at the clothesline. Our original thought had been to fire a shot over Vicky's head, just to show her we weren't scared of her. But then another opportunity presented itself.

Vicky had placed the basket on the ground and was bending over to get out a big, wet double sheet. Her back was to us. The target, clad in pink Bermuda shorts as I recall, was just too tempting. We quickly recalibrated the range and elevation, loaded a round and fired.

SMACK! Direct hit, right in the middle of the butt.

She whooped and jumped and dropped the sheet onto the ground. Then, wheeling around to face us, she stepped on it, grinding dirt and grass into it with the sole of her sneaker. And we shot her again, in the stomach.

Of course, she ran into the house and told on us. And it was that afternoon that P.D. and I got out first lesson from Mom on how to wash sheets and how much bleach to use to remove a grass stain in the shape of a girl's tennis shoe. And our cannon went onto a high shelf, where we could not reach it, for a month.

But it was worth it to P.D. and me. The look on Vicky's face, when she turned around and saw that cannon barrel poking out of the bushes, more than made up for losing our artillery for a month. Call us morons, will she?

You know, I really think it was a golden age, my kidhood. Then again, I think all kidhoods can be golden ages. There is never a better time to be a human being on this planet, and I get a lump in my throat thinking of the kids—and I know they're out there—who don't have a kidhood as fun as mine. There are kids out there right now who are literally fighting for their lives, at an age when they should be fighting with their sisters as P.D. and I did.

But while we are tempted to think of kidhood in terms of play or toys or candy or television, I think the real gold comes from someplace much, much deeper.

I realize now that kidhood was the last time I really relied on intuition to make my way through the world. As I have gotten older I have acquired layers, layers of knowledge, to be sure, but also layers of guilt and anger and hurt and suspicion and a hundred other conditions that affect the way I see, and deal with, the world.

In kidhood, my needs would be met by someone else: parents, teachers, grandparents, adults, and I was sheltered from harm. I was secure of my place, in class, in the family, at the dinner table, and that made it possibly for me to simply live my life without worry and with an endless open imagination. I could use my mind to turn a basement stairwell into a submarine or a fort or a foxhole, completely and utterly. When we were in it and our minds were open to play, that is what it became and it was as real to me then as is the desk I see in front of me now. Which is the way kids are supposed to live: freely, intuitively, happily.

That is what Albert and Edwin did, in a way, in the Golden Age of Copyboys. They might not have had the intellectual horsepower of the reporters and editors they served, but neither did they have the ulcers and migraines, the anger, the suspicion, the fear that you acquire in the process known as growing up.

In my office I keep several toys: my old Jerry Mahoney ventriloquist figure, some electric trains, a little rubber dog that squeaks, which Mom says was my very first plaything. None, however, is more meaningful to me than a beat-up Mattel Fanner Fifty that now sits on a shelf near the telephone. Every once in a while I pick it up to feel its heft. Occasionally I give it a twirl or two on my index finger. I get again a tiny little sliver of what it felt like to grow up in the Golden Age of Kidhood.

~ School Days. ~

In which we make the acquaintance of Monty Jo Strawer, the best friend a teenage guy ever had, and I stun the world of science . . .

By the time I got to junior high school, I no longer loved school. Neither did I hate it, though. I simply saw it as a part of the Natural Order of Things, like sunrise or breathing. Adults drank martinis, stayed up late and went to work. Kids drank Kool-Aid, had bedtimes, and went to school. And that was that. It was just the way the world was arranged.

That's not to say there weren't parts of the school day I loved, and also parts I hated. Music, reading, social studies I loved. Some days (when we played baseball, for example, or gym hockey) I loved phys-Ed. Other days (basketball, gymnastics) I hated it. Same with art. When we drew pictures, I loved it. When we did "projects" involving construction paper, scissors and white paste—which seemed to be ninety percent of elementary school art—I hated it.

Math and science, I hated. What's more, I think they hated me. They sure seemed to when report cards came around.

In one of those Great Cosmic Jokes that only come along every dozen or so lifetimes, I had the bad fortune to attend school when the United States was locked in a Space Race with the Soviet Union.

Things had gotten off to a bad start for the home team with the Soviet Union's launching of Sputnik, a little beeping satellite, 22 inches in circumference, on Oct. 4, 1957. America had no beeping globe in space.

One way America responded was by putting new emphasis on math and science in school curricula, the objective being to raise a new generation of Einsteins with which to do technobattle with the Russians.

Then I came along and threw a wrench into the works.

Oh, I did all right at first. Arithmetic didn't give me too many problems. I wasn't even all that befuddled when I got a little older and suddenly found that arithmetic had given way to mathematics, which as we all know is Greek for "harder arithmetic."

Along about junior high, though, I began to struggle. Algebra made no sense to me. Geometry wasn't any better. And I certainly wasn't gaining any academic ground in science, except in the area of frog dissection. For some reason, I had a real talent for pinning frogs to a little pan of formaldehyde-treated wax, and slicing them open with a scalpel. Had there been more call for it, I might have gone into frog-dissecting for a living. That's how good I was.

My scientific bright spot, one that amazes my family to this day, was in agriculture class. I, a kid who had heretofore shown absolutely no interest in the practice, much less the study of agrictulture, made straight A's.

I think I know why I found the course so interesting. Up until that point, my Uncle John, one of Mom's older brothers, a farmer, seemed to regard me with something between impatience and outright scorn. This bothered me, because truth be told, I admired Uncle John a great deal and wanted him to think well of me.

My first reaction was typical for a kid of my age—about thirteen then, I guess. I acted like a moron. The less he seemed to think of me, the more obnoxious I became—smart-mouthed, flippant, temperamental. I gave him the whole thirteen-year-old Attitude Arsenal.

But when I started studying agriculture, which, to be honest, I took simply because all my friends were taking it and I had a hole in my schedule, I suddenly found that I had something I could talk about with Uncle John. It began when I needed help with a homework assignment about legumes. Uncle John, a brilliant man who never made less than an A during his entire time at Purdue University, responded with a half-hour lecture about legumes which I more or less regurgitated verbatim on my paper. Result: A.

Well, that was it. From then on, Uncle John and I were bonded by agriculture, and we remained that way until he died.

When I entered high school, I encountered new levels of math and science in which I would not be interested, an experience which achieved its zenith in chemistry class my junior year.

Now, it wasn't completely my fault. I think the teacher, Mr. Adams, deserves some of the blame, too. It was he, after all, who bore a striking resemblance to Dr. Julius Kelp as portrayed by Jerry Lewis in *The Nutty Professor*. I'm not kidding. Thick glasses, buck teeth, slightly absent-minded—this guy was a ringer for Dr. Julius Kelp.

I thought that the second I clapped eyes on him and I was never able to get it out of my mind. Consequently, I didn't pay much attention to the guy. I was too busy laughing at him behind my chemistry book.

I scraped by with B's and C's for the first semester, but after Christmas break my interest in chemistry—scant to begin with—evaporated completely. The first grading period, I got a D. And since I was the kid who was never content to leave well enough alone, I worked extra hard the next grading period and managed to get the grade reduced to an F—the first of my life. I was in deep trouble, and facing the prospect of having to repeat the whole obnoxious affair in my senior year, when Mr. Adams inadvertently threw me a life preserver: The Science Fair.

"Class, I have an announcement." I look up from my chemistry book, which I hadn't been reading anyway, to see what sort of torture Mr. Adams has planned for me today. To the rest of the class, it's a project or a quiz but to me, with my inability to grasp even the fundamentals of chemistry, it's torture.

"I'm going to give you a choice," he says, waving a sheaf of mimeographed papers in the air. "This next class period, you can enter a project in the School Science Fair and have it count for two-thirds of your final, semester grade. Or you can take the chemistry final."

It takes me about two seconds to make up my mind. This is what we call a no-brainer. I am entering the science fair.

I take the sheet handed to me and looked over the list of areas in which I could enter: Biology (no), Chemistry (ABSOLUTELY not), Math (get real), Physics (you must be kidding). And then my eye falls on Earth and Space Science.

Bingo.

Why Earth and Space Science? Simple. All the other kids are talking about doing chemistry projects. Nobody mentions Earth and Space Science. This, I reason, will improve my chances of getting a ribbon and salvaging my crummy chemistry grade.

Without knowing it, I then make a brilliant decision. I decide that my Earth and Space Science exhibit will be something to do with my old pal, agriculture.

The brilliance of this—unknown to me at the the time, mind you—is that every other kid who enters Earth and Space Science will skip the Earth part completely and concentrate on Space, which in terms of the Science Fair means he will dig out his old Model Rocket project from 4-H Club and enter it, as is. My earthbound, agricultural project will stand out from the crowd simply because it isn't about rockets.

Not that I know this. At the time, I'm just looking for something easy.

After carefully thinking it over for three entire minutes, I decide my project will be in the field of agronomy, the science of soil management. Why? I like the sound of it. Agronomy. Anything that ends in "onomy" is going to seem a lot more sophisticated than model rockets.

I decide to conduct soil tests at various farms around the neighborhood (ours, Grandpa's, the neighbors') and then make recommendations on crop plantings and soil treatments accordingly. I will be careful and apply sound judgment and reasoning. And if I run into trouble, I'll ask Uncle John what he recommends.

I borrow a soil-testing kit from the agriculture department, take it home and promptly forget about it until two days before the science fair.

Hurriedly I collect my soil samples, put them into test tubes with the reagents, read the soil pH results according to the scale on the inside of the testing box lid, and make a few meaningless recommendations about planting alternative crops (blueberries, I recall was one of them) and fertilizing regimens.

I then cobble together a display from three small pieces of pegboard. I type my findings and attach them to the boards, place some test tubes, dirt and chemicals in front of the thing, and my science fair project is done. With no time to spare, I haul it to the high school and set it up on a table in the gym.

And son-of-a-gun if I didn't win a blue ribbon.

The judge, however, tells me that my display is too dumpy, too small and colorless. If I want to compete at the next level—the Regional Science Fair, over at Tri-State College in Angola—he says I will have to build something bigger, brighter and more eye-catching.

Of course, I pay no attention. I got my blue ribbon at the local science fair and that's good enough to get my grade up to a gentleman's C. I'm satisfied. I have no intention of taking this scam any further.

The next day in class, Mr. Adams drops the bomb: Anyone who competes in the Regional Science Fair will get extra credit that will be applied to his semester grade, based on how he finishes. "Now, you blue ribbon winners," he says, "should realize that this will be a very difficult competition compared to the one we just had. You'll be going up against blue ribbon winners from every high school in northeastern Indiana. Don't think you can just waltz over there and win because you won here." He's looking at me as he says that last part.

I don't care. Extra credit? It's No-Brainer No. 2. I sign up.

Again, I wait until the last minute to start my project. The night before the Regional, I do what all kids do when they are faced with an impossible school task on a tight deadline: I yell for Mom.

She wastes no time. She rummages around the cellar and comes up with three twelve-by-thirty-six pieces of pegboard. She mounts them together with hinges and then cuts letters (A, G, R, O, N, O, M, Y) from red construction paper. While I retype my reports, Mom puts together a display that is nothing short of spectacular—big, bright and eye-catching, just like the man said.

The next morning, a Saturday, we load it into the car and drive over to Tri-State. I find the room where the Earth and Space Science projects are being set up, and once again find that I am virtually the only Earthbound competitor. Every president of every junior rocketry club in northeastern Indiana has a rocket display in there. And then there's me and my dirt.

I suppose this is as good a time as any to mention that the judges in the Earth and Space Science division came to us from the faculties of Purdue and Michigan State universities. The agriculture faculties.

When the Purdue judge comes around to talk with me about my project, he asks what I plan to do after high school.

"Go to Purdue to study agriculture," I say, cheerfully.

A few minutes later, the Michigan State judge asks me the same question.

"Go to Michigan State to study agriculture," I say, again cheerfully.

Of course, I am lying through my teeth. The truthful answer to "What do you plan to do after high school?" is "I haven't the faintest idea." The only colleges I had ever considered going to are Indiana University and the University of Notre Dame, and if I was going to study anything, which seems unlikely, it would probably be journalism.

But I want a ribbon, and I don't care what I have to say to get it.

Turns out I get one, too. A blue one. First place.

The school gets a plaque with my name on it, which I present to Mr. Adams on Monday. To say he is stunned is to put it mildly. All of the science geeks, the ones who had entered chemistry experiments, the ones who got A's in his class, had been skunked. I, the one who was bringing up the rear in the class standings, was the only one who got a blue ribbon.

"You?" he keeps saying. "You?"

My chemistry grade that semester works out to a B-plus. It would have been an A but there was no ignoring that F on the books—the one that indicates I have absolutely no understanding of the material and no interest in acquiring any. I don't mind. A B-plus is beyond my wildest dreams.

But even more satisfying is being able to walk down the hall of

Lakeland High School every day to see that plaque with my name on it—Mike Redmond, Regional Science Fair Winner, Agronomy Whiz and Con Man Extraordinaire.

※ ※ ※

Actually, my lack of interest in science and math was just a symptom of a greater condition that afflicted me in my high school years: a lack of interest in school, period. Oh, I did well enough in music, English and speech to make it look like I was still an active student, but under the façade of a middling-good student there lived a kid who attended school mostly because it gave him a chance to hang out with his best friend, Monty Jo Strawser.

Monty—or Jo, as I called him—was my boon companion, my brother of a different mother, my inseparable pal back then.

We had hooked up in the eighth grade, when I was the new kid in Brighton School. It was about six weeks into the school year when the civics teacher, Boyd Grove, attempted to engage us in a discussion about race relations in America.

My classmates, not a single one of whom had ever seen another person who wasn't white except on television, spouted all kinds of ignorance about how Negroes were shiftless and lazy and good-for-nothing—and some of them weren't even that polite. This made me mad. I was raised by parents who taught me that skin color makes absolutely no difference and that each person on the planet deserved to be judged on his own merit. To do otherwise, they said, was simply wrong and would not be tolerated in our house.

And so I raised my hand and launched into a speech about how nobody in this class full of goobers knew what they were talking about, that I was the only person in the room who had ever even MET a Negro and they were all, to put it bluntly, a bunch of boobs.

Mr. Grove tried to jump in with some comments about how yes, he was certain that most black people were fine but Stokely Carmichael (Stokey, he pronounced it) and H. Rap Brown were troublemakers and just made things worse for everybody.

At which point I lit into him too, about how if he had ever seen the conditions under which some people were forced to live in Washington, D.C.—our nation's capital and the city I had recently come from—he might understand why the anger of Stoke-LY Carmichael and H. Rap Brown made some sense. A fiery little liberal I was.

The bell rang and between classes I went to the boys' room. I was standing there doing what you do when Monty Jo Strawser, with whom I had barely exchanged more than a greeting, went to the next stall.

"There's the guy who argues with Boyd Grove," he said.

And a legendary friendship was born.

From then on, it was an unusual day that did not find us hanging out together. And the older we got, the worse it got. Or better, from my point of view.

It reached its zenith in high school when Jo and I were embroiled in a number of adventures. The most famous came to be known in LaGrange County lore as Skunk Night.

It's Friday afternoon in Mr. Potter's American History class. As luck would have it, I am sitting next to Monty Jo, who is behind our good friend, Larry "Elmo" Rowe, who got his nickname one night when we were talking about Amish people, which LaGrange County has in abundance.

"What I can't understand," Larry said, "is how an Amish mother could look down at a sweet, innocent, cute little baby, all pink and cuddly and adorable, and say, 'Your name's gonna be Elmo.'" From then on, we hardly ever called him anything else.

As the clock ticks down to the end of the school day, Mr. Potter's class—never the strictest educational atmosphere, owing to Mr. Potter's preference for telling bad jokes than teaching history—descends into Social Hour. Monty Jo and Elmo turn to me and say, "Shall we go out and raise some havoc tonight?"

"Why yes," I reply. "Let's do. Havoc-raising is what we do best."

We don't raise BAD havoc. We never hurt anybody or cause a great deal of property damage. We are partial to goofy fun-type havoc.

Throwing water balloons at the sophomore class float for the home-coming parade. Parking at the A&W with a bucket of chicken from Colonel Sanders, ordering small root beers to go with it, and throwing the chicken bones out the car windows. Stealing county road signs (my own personal triumph includes taking County Road 00 by County Road 00 right from the center of town).

A few hours later, Jo wheels into the driveway in his two-tone (green and white) 1955 Chevy. I jump in and we drive the twelve miles to LaGrange to pick up Elmo and create our havoc. We have half a tank of gas, two packages of cheap cigars, and a grand total of about seven bucks among the three of us. We're good to go.

"Where first?" asks Elmo.

"Railroad bridge," says Jo. "The train's due."

This means he has to go to the bathroom.

There was a railroad bridge north of town, a steep wooden affair shaped like an inverted "V" over the north-south B&O line. We boys considered it one of the best places in the entire county to take a leak. Don't ask me why. I think it might have been simply because we were morons.

Anyway, we drive out to the bridge and Jo does his business. We climb back into the car and begin driving toward LaGrange when we spy upon the road a freshly killed, still-warm, stinking-to-high-heaven skunk.

We stop the car and get out to look at it. It looks peaceful, lying there on the road. Cute, almost. And once you get used to it, the smell isn't even all that bad.

"I've got an idea," says Jo.

He trots to the car and extracts from the trunk a length of thin white rope known locally as Kirsch cord, because it was made for Kirsch drapery hardware, manufactured just up the road in Sturgis, Michigan. Every car in LaGrange County had a coil of Kirsch cord in the trunk. It was handy stuff.

Without a word, Jo ties one end to the dead skunk's tail and the other end to the bumper of his Chevy. "Get in," he says.

The plan is simply to drive around LaGrange dragging this skunk behind us. That, we figure, will be outrageous enough to get us talked about at school the next Monday. And so we drive up and down the streets of the town, waving to our friends and acting like we did not know what we were towing.

As we detour through a residential neighborhood, though, we notice something unusual. We are being followed by dogs. Lots of dogs. Every loose dog in the town of LaGrange, it seems.

They have picked up the scent of that skunk and now we had a pack of at least a dozen running behind us, barking and howling.

We laugh so hard I think we may have to go out to the railroad bridge again. And then Jo is seized by a brilliant idea.

He turns the wheel, gives it the gas, outdistances the dogs and drives to Mr. Potter's house. We get out and knock on the door. Mr. Potter answers.

"Hi, Mr. Potter!" Jo says. "I'm thinking about selling my car and thought you might want to buy it."

"Well, I . . ."

"Really, it's a good car. You'd like it."

"Yes, but . . ."

"Oh, come on. Let's take it for a drive."

Jo throws him the keys and he and Mr. Potter head out to the car. Mr. Potter settles behind the wheel and away they go, tires squealing, gravel flying.

And here come the dogs.

Mr. Potter rounds a corner and the pack of canines go after him, baying and howling, ears flapping, feet slipping on the gravel. Larry and I are laughing so hard we can't stay upright. We fall down in Mr. Potter's yard, clutching our sides and rolling around in the grass with tears coming to our eyes.

We can hear the Chevy roaring and screeching around the block. We can hear the dogs yelping. And we can just imagine Monty Jo there in the passenger seat, laughing his head off, while unsuspecting Mr. Potter steers the wheel and hits the pedals.

In a couple of minutes Mr. Potter comes skidding back down the street. He whips the car into a parking space and gets out. The dogs come running up behind and congregate around the skunk, although Mr. Potter seems not to notice.

"Well, boys," he says, "the steering is a little loose and the brakes are lousy. You might want to get those worked on before you try to sell it."

He walks toward his front door and turns around.

"Oh, and get rid of the skunk."

It is a full five minutes before we can stop laughing and compose ourselves enough to drive away and do what Mr. Potter tells us to do, get rid of the skunk. Which we do. We leave it under a LaGrange County Sheriff's Department squad car.

And then, our havoc well and truly raised, we head home to think about what we can do when we go back out on Saturday night. Not that we'll be able to top ourselves. We already know that Skunk Night will be the No. 1 topic of conversation when school starts up again on Monday morning.

※ ※ ※

Along about the middle of my junior year of high school, my interest in academics began to wane. Oh, who are we kidding? It dried up and blew away. I had done a little figuring and had determined that, thanks to my practice of never taking a study hall but instead filling the gaps in my schedule with classes, I had already piled up more than enough credits to graduate under Indiana state law.

Since I had already achieved what I had come to high school to do, I decided to coast through my last year. I lightened my load considerably.

I only had two "solid"—that is, non-elective—classes my senior year: Senior English and government/economics. I barely got through them.

Senior English was English Literature. I loved American Literature and made good grades in it, but English Lit bored me to tears. It began with *Beowulf* and went downhill from there. By the time we got to Shakespeare, I was squeaking by on glibness. I failed every quiz, but I always got A's on my themes. Actually, this turned out to be valuable preparation for my later life as a newspaper columnist.

Government and economics, a class I had actually looked forward to once, was an unmitigated disaster. The teacher was a short guy by the name of Mr. Rodegheiro, whom we instantly renamed "Rodent." The first day of class—the very first day—he endeavored to tell us about a free market economy as compared to other systems, and told us we could—and I am not making this up—"analytically analyze it on a linear line."

That was the exact moment I lost interest in his class.

What kept me coming to school—besides the fact that all my friends were there—were the classes I enjoyed: band, stage band (we got to play what we thought was jazz and believed ourselves to be VERY cool), and journalism. My senior year, I was the exalted editor of Lakeland's weekly newspaper, *The Echo*.

Well, it was supposed to be weekly. Upon becoming editor, I set about getting my friends to sign up for the newspaper staff, and in doing so loaded the roster with guys who were fun to hang out with and who occasionally, very occasionally, wrote something. Monty Jo, for instance. I think he wrote one story the entire year, a profile of one of the janitors that began, "Omer the janitor started out like we all did, as a child."

The result of it all was we blew deadlines with alarming regularity, and under my leadership, if you can call it that, what had once been a weekly, started coming out every 10 days, and then every two weeks, and finally, at the end of the year, once a month.

Journalism class gave us one opportunity not enjoyed by many other kids at Lakeland High School: the chance to leave the building during the school day. Lakeland was a closed campus. Once you got there in the morning, you had to stay there until you were dismissed, but journalism kids got a special dispensation to go out into the community to sell advertising.

Which, of course, we took advantage of shamelessly, although we didn't sell ads as much as we sat around Dee's Newsstand drinking nickel Cokes (10 cents if you wanted them flavored with cherry or lemon syrup) and sneaking peeks at the nudie books on the top shelf of the magazine rack.

Journalism class was the middle class of three in the afternoon. By (ahem) coincidence, my first class of the afternoon was a study hall—as it was for Monty Jo, Larry Rowe, Jeff Mead and Mike Pipher; all the pals I had talked into taking journalism.

That meant we could leave the school at the start of lunch period, 11:30 AM, grab a cheap lunch downtown (a chili dog, potato chips and small Coke set you back less than 50 cents at the Dairy Queen) and goof off until 1:25 PM, when we were supposed to be back at our desks, typing our stories, although we occasionally stretched that to 2:00 or 2:15. Out there trying to sell ads, you know.

Now, just up the road from us was Sturgis, Michigan, where you could buy beer at the age of eighteen. It wasn't long before we began heading that way to get a six-pack of whatever was cheap at a little liquor store we called "Dirty Mary's." Then we would come back to school and sit there, slightly gassed, while the others in journalism class, we thought, admired our derring-do. "Jeeminy, you guys smell like a brewery" was considered a high compliment in our world.

For a while, we even had a thriving bootleg business. Howe Military School, which was even more of a closed campus than ours, was halfway between Lakeland and Dirty Mary's. We knew some of the cadets there, and would arrange to pick up beer for them, which we would deliver to the back of the campus. We always charged an outrageous markup, of course, usually in the neighborhood of 500 percent, but what could they do? It was a seller's market. Besides, they were all rich kids from Detroit and Chicago. They could afford it.

I think about this now and realize how much I squandered that last year of school. I was getting a free education which I more or less booted. My class ranking slipped from somewhere around fifteenth to somewhere around twenty-fifth, all in a year, and it had long range effects. I spent the next several years trying to make up the gaps.

I taught myself English Literature by reading, and while I never grew to love Shakespeare, I did learn to admire his work. I still don't like *Beowulf*, though.

I taught myself government and economics by reading the newspaper and participating as a voter and a consumer. In my own defense, however, I must say that I developed a fairly good understanding of the differences between a market economy and a closed economy without having to analytically analyze it on a linear line.

But something I DID learn in high school, something that could not be taught from a book, has stood me well over time. I learned the value of friendship. I learned what it was like to be in a pack of buddies who wanted to do nothing more than have a good time without hurting anyone. I learned that fun is as important a component to your education as reading, writing and arithmetic.

And I learned how to find the places with the lowest prices on beer.

◟ Fun and/or Games, Part II. ◞

*And now, without further adieu, please welcome the Redmond
girls: Amy The Kid Sister and Vicky The Enforcer . . .*

I *wouldn't want you thinking I spent my entire kidhood* picking on my
brother, P.D., because I didn't. I also had two sisters.

Actually, I can't recall a single time my kid sister Amy and I ever
tangled, about anything. Amy is twelve years younger than I and from
the very beginning she and I have been devoted to one another. In
many respects, we're the most-alike of any two of the children in the
family.

It was a wonderful thing to be a twelve-year-old boy with a baby
sister. Amy brought out a gentle side in me and, I suspect, in that way
helped to tame the Raging Hormone Years of my early teens. Nothing
takes the fight out of you like the adoring glance of a blond, blue-eyed
toddler, who just happens to think you hung the moon.

I learned a lot being the big brother. I learned to change diapers,
warm bottles, and spoon baby food into a reluctant mouth. I learned
how to rock a baby to sleep, and how to burp her when her stomach
was upset. Maybe that's the reason I never had kids. I already did all
that stuff. Bought the ticket, rode the ride and I have the baby-barf-
stained T-shirt to show for it.

With Amy I also became a teacher. I was the one who taught her
to tie her shoes and snap her fingers. And my brother will never forget
the day I taught her a special trick, just for him.

He came home from basketball practice to find me sitting on the
front steps. Amy sat next to me. She was all of about three years old, I

think, and P.D. felt much the same about her then as I did. She was our adorable, little baby sister, the sweet, innocent presence that had come to us to make our lives better.

As he approached us, I whispered to Amy, "OK. Now."

Whereupon she raised a chubby little fist and gave him the finger. "Look what Mikey taught me," she said.

"Let's go show Mommy what Mikey taught you," said P.D. Spoilsport.

I got my driver's license when Amy was four, and used to love to take her for rides. I will admit, however, that my motives were not entirely honorable. I knew that if I took Amy with me to the Dairy Queen in LaGrange on a Sunday afternoon, any girl in the place would find her irresistible and I would have all the female company I could handle. It worked, too. Every time. Amy and I would sit down—me with a Coke, she with her baby cone. In seconds, every girl in the place would be flocking to our table to "ooh" and "ah" over my pretty little sister. I was shameless.

After I got my license, I was the one who took Amy to the movies whenever a kiddie show came to the Strand Theater, just over the state line in Sturgis. We saw *Willie Wonka and the Chocolate Factory*. We saw *Chitty-Chitty Bang-Bang*. And of course all the Disney movies—*Cinderella, Snow White, Sleeping Beauty, Pinocchio, Dumbo . . . .*

Oh, *Dumbo*. *Dumbo* was a tough one for me.

It was a matinée, and I think I was the oldest person there. I would estimate the average age of the rest of the audience at four-and-one-half. I know for certain that as I looked down the theater toward the screen, all I could see of the other patrons were the tops of their little heads peeking up over the backs of the seats.

Amy and I settled in with our popcorn and candy and the matinée began—a Mickey Mouse cartoon first, followed by a True Life Adventure short subject. Then came the feature, *Dumbo*.

I was fine through the opening credits. I was fine through the first part of the movie, when Dumbo was born, when his giant ears were revealed, when the other elephants made fun of him.

But then came the scene where the kids teased him and his mother got mad and was locked up as a mad elephant, and the little mouse took Dumbo to visit her in confinement. Through the bars she rocked Dumbo in her trunk while a chorus sang, "Baby Mine." I could feel myself starting to go.

Then came the scene I had been dreading. It was time for Dumbo to leave, and neither he nor his mother wanted to say goodbye. They intertwined their trunks lovingly, as Dumbo moved away, hanging on for those last, sweet blessed moments of contact until finally, excruciatingly, they were touching only with the tips. And then they let go.

So did I.

The tears I had felt welling up in my eyes now cascaded down my cheeks. I took a deep, shuddering breath. I sniffled. I didn't care that I was sixteen years old, almost a man. I was bawling like a baby.

I felt Amy's little hand on my shoulder. I glanced down. She was staring at me with a look of real concern on her face.

"It'll be OK, Mikey," she assured me.

And then she held out her popcorn.

※ ※ ※

I tried to be as good a big brother as I could to Amy. I included her in everything I could. When I got my first motorcycle—a Honda 350—Amy rode to school on the back of it, wearing P.D.'s old junior-high football helmet for protection. She was the only first-grader who came to school that way. It made her quite a celebrity.

My friends loved Amy, too. Not the least of these was Monty Jo. He was an only child, and I think he got a charge out of being around and having fun with someone so much younger. He and Amy watched cartoons together, played Candy Land together, ate snacks together. Jo took her for rides on his horse, Cap. He even invited her to his sixteenth birthday party. She was the smallest person there and as much the guest of honor as was the birthday boy himself.

Amy reciprocated with nothing short of pure love. She even announced when she was six that when she grew up she was going to marry Monty Jo. She meant it, too.

But I was Amy's champion. Which is as good a way as any to begin telling you about my relationship with my older sister, Vicky.

Vicky and I enjoy a good sibling relationship now, but some people will have you believe that we never got along when we were kids. This is absurd. At first, we got along great. Of course, I didn't do much more than drool back then, but that's beside the point.

After P.D. was born, there was a shift in the family dynamic. Vicky was now officially outnumbered by brothers. However, her age—four years older than I, seven older than P.D.—more than addressed this imbalance. In fact, Vicky became Mom's trusted lieutenant, her enforcer, her Duly Appointed Representative. "Vicky, keep an eye on The Boys" was usually the last thing Mom said before leaving the house on an errand.

P.D. and I were given to understand by Mom that Vicky was the perfect child. We didn't believe it, of course, but Vicky did, and she reminded us of it every chance she got. She kept her room neat. She did her homework on time and got good grades. She was helpful around the house.

In our younger days, that wasn't much of a problem. Vicky was bigger than we were and we weren't inclined to tangle with her. We were too busy fighting among ourselves.

About the only time things ever got out of hand was when Mom and Dad were at a going-away party. Dad had taken the job with the congressman and his newspaper colleagues were sending him off in newspaper style, which meant a lot of drinking and dirty jokes at somebody's house.

Our house was on the market and the real estate agent had a customer sniffing around and we kids were under special orders to be on our Best Behavior—i.e., don't break any windows, write on the walls, set fire to the living room—until the deal closed.

When the folks left that night, with Vicky in charge of us boys, we had a pizza and watched a little TV and then, for some reason,

Vicky and I got into a fight.

I don't remember what it was about. All I do remember is that at one point Vicky started chasing me. I ran up the stairs to my room, slammed the door and held it closed as Vicky pounded on it and yelled for me to open up and get the beating I had coming. Naturally, I declined. This made Vicky so mad she kicked the door.

And put her foot right through it.

The tension drained out of the atmosphere immediately. Whatever it was we had been fighting about no longer mattered. There was a hole in the door—the door that the folks were trying to sell along with the rest of the house.

P.D. and I went to bed shortly after that. I didn't sleep, though. I couldn't. There was a hole in the door, put there by my sister's big foot. I wanted to see what happened when the folks got home and found out Perfect Vicky wasn't so Perfect after all.

I didn't have long to wait. Lying in my bed, I heard the Pontiac crunching over the stones in our driveway. I heard my Dad and Mom chatting as they came up the walk. I heard the door open.

And then I heard my sister—who up to this point had been quiet as a churchmouse—begin to sob uncontrollably.

The folks asked her what was wrong.

"Mike . . . the door!" she wailed.

Uh-oh.

I heard my father's clomping angrily up the stairs, his footsteps pausing just outside my room as he assessed the damage. I decided that my best defense—my only defense—would be to feign sleep. Maybe if he saw me sleeping, I thought, he would give me a reprieve and wait until morning to kill me.

Nope. The next thing I knew I was levitating out of my bed. Dad caught me in mid-air and pinned me to the wall. He was furious.

"What," he seethed, "did you do to the door?"

Me? I didn't do anything to the door except close it. Vicky was the one who put her foot through it.

"Nothing," I said.

That was the wrong answer.

I have heard it said that people who undergo great shock some-times develop a gap in their memory about it. They don't remember the auto accident in which they were injured, let's say, or can't quite recall how they got out of the burning building. It's nature's way, I suppose, of protecting us from having to live over and over again through a devastating personal experience.

So it is with me and the rest of that night. I have no clear recol-lection of what happened to me. I presume I was spanked. I presume I got a lecture about how the parents were trying to sell the house and I may well have derailed the deal. I presume, but I can't say for certain because I simply do not remember.

What I do remember is glancing over while Dad had me pinned to the wall and seeing Mom standing in the doorway with her arm around my still-sobbing sister. And then I remember Vicky's eyes rais-ing to meet mine. And I remember the faintest hint of a smile curling around Vicky's lips.

As we got into our teens, the disagreements between us came more frequently, as P.D. and I became less inclined to respect Vicky's authority. Well, in my case at least, I was less inclined to respect ANY authority. Vicky's was part of a long list of authority figures I was no longer paying attention to, including teachers, police officers and Dad. Mom, yes; but Dad, no.

The addition of Amy to the mix changed the dynamic yet again, although not in the way you might expect simply by reading the scorecard (two boys *vs.* two girls). It created shifting lineups within the family. There were the three older kids—Vicky, me and P.D.—and then the newcomer, Amy. There were the three younger kids—me, P.D. and Amy—and the older sister, Vicky. Vicky and I, by virtue of our older status, had memories of a time when P.D. and Amy did not exist, which created yet another lineup. P.D. and Amy, the younger kids, had inter-ests that meant nothing to Vicky and me. And on and on.

And then there was the bond between Amy and me—the baby sister and the big brother—which came into play one summer afternoon when she was about three, I was fifteen and Vicky was nineteen and home from college.

Amy had done something—spilled her juice, I think—and Vicky was chastising her for it, far too vehemently in my view. And so I stepped in and told Vicky, in my most diplomatic way, to knock it off and pick on someone her own size. OK, so maybe I wasn't diplomatic. Maybe I made my case quite forcefully. It has been known to happen.

Well, Vicky blew a fuse. She was like Dad in that way, quick to anger and completely comfortable with expressing it. In this case, expressing it meant coming after me, looking for a fight. She tried to slap me.

As you might expect, I didn't feel like being slapped right then, so I grabbed her wrists. This made her all the madder. She squirmed free and quickly switched to her weapon of choice: her fingernails.

She came at me with claws bared. I remember thinking at the time that it was the exact same pose used by Margaret Hamilton as the Wicked Witch of the West in *The Wizard of Oz*—fingers spread and crooked with those blade-like nails at the tips.

She sunk them into my forearm.

I didn't much care for that.

I hauled off and popped her one on the shoulder. Vicky staggered back a few paces and came at me again with those nails, looking to carve me up. I deflected her attack and popped her on the other shoulder.

This just made her madder. She got up a head of steam and charged.

Amy, who had been watching all of this in rapt fascination, piped up: "Get her, Mikey!"

So I balled up a fist and threw a sharp right. It sailed between Vicky's hands—she didn't know a thing about boxing—and landed squarely on her chin. Down she went.

P.D., who had been sitting there trying to watch television all this time, said, "Nice shot." And that was the end of the fight. Amy and I left Vicky in a crumpled heap on the living room floor, and went out to the kitchen for more juice.

A couple of hours later, Mom came home. Vicky, as was her practice whenever we had a fight, met Mom in the driveway and started in with a wailing litany of complaints and grievances. I had attacked her for no reason, she said, and beaten her severely about the head and shoulders, and on and on and on.

Nine times out of ten, this would have been a good idea. Vicky, after all, was Mom's trusted lieutenant, her enforcer, her Duly Appointed Representative. More than once I caught holy what-for simply because I wasn't quick enough to get to the driveway before Vicky did. Then again, it probably wouldn't have made any difference. Mom tended to believe whatever Vicky told her.

So Vicky wailed and cried and complained and Mom, true to form, got mad and came into the house looking for me. Vicky trailed close behind. I could see that curl of a smile forming on her lips again.

Mom was lighting into me about all that Vicky said I had done when my brother came strolling in from the living room.

"That's not the way it happened," he said.

Mom stopped and turned to him. "Then tell me what happened," she demanded.

And so he did. He told her that Vicky had started it, that I was just stepping in because she was being too harsh with Amy, and that Vicky had blown a fuse and I had no choice but to defend myself.

I showed her my arm with the claw marks on it.

She believed us and Vicky got one of Mom's legendary chewing-outs, Mom Speech No. 8113, "You Are The Oldest And I By-God Expect You To Act Like An Adult."

It was a moment of delicious victory for me, and might have been for P.D., too, had he not made the mistake of going outside later, after Mom had left the house to go over to Grandma and Grandpa's.

He was sitting on the back steps of our house, minding his own business, when he heard a "click" behind him. He got up and found the door had been locked.

He ran to the front of the house. That door was locked, too. He jumped off the front porch steps and raced around to the side door, the last of three entry ways to the house.

Through the glass of the door he saw Vicky. As he reached for the knob, she turned the lock. Then she gave him the finger and walked away.

As the years have gone by, Vicky and I have grown closer. She married a wonderful guy, Steve, and settled down to raise two beautiful daughters, Amanda and Gillian, and to work as a school teacher in Garrett, Indiana. Now, when we see each other, we truly enjoy each other's company. We laugh and joke and enjoy a brother-sister relationship that is as good as any I know. When Steve was diagnosed with cancer of the esophagus and stomach, requiring a marathon surgery and a long recovery period, my sister reacted with strength and calm that was a marvel to behold. I love her, and not only that, I like her. And more than any other time in my life, I am proud to be Vicky's brother.

And I am proud to be Amy's. The only rough patch Amy and I ever had was when she was in the Army, in Germany, and called us one to day to report that she had eloped and was now the wife of Sgt. John Carpenter, a man we had never met. I was steamed. Dad was in the last months of his life, and the last thing the family needed was the drama of Amy's elopement on top of it.

Dad died and we had the funeral without her. She had already used up her emergency leave a few months before, when he was close to death but didn't take the final step. In my head I understood why Amy couldn't be there, but in my heart I thought it was wrong that we buried Dad and she wasn't there.

Amy and I didn't have much to say for a while. Mom kept me up to date on her, and when Amy had a baby girl, Erin, she sent me pictures, but I didn't go out of my way to get back to her.

Then Mom told me Amy and the baby were coming to the States. Her plane would land in Indianapolis and I was supposed to pick them up. I went out to the airport and when I saw my sister walking off the plane with that little pink bundle, I melted. I grabbed the baby from her, hugged them both, and that was the end of the only time Amy and I ever didn't get along.

Amy gave birth shortly afterward to a boy, Noah, who reminds me an awful lot of a couple of guys I used to know. He's nuts for basketball like his Uncle P.D., and he's crazy for electric trains like his Uncle Mike. He's also kind of a smart aleck, although I don't know where he got that.

Probably from his mom and his Aunt Vicky.

·⤙ We Gather Together. ⤚·

Please pass the turkey, the potatoes, the dressing, the gravy,
the . . . oh, heck . . . just give me some of everything!

It has been said that of all the things that trigger memory, none is stronger than the sense of smell. That has certainly been the case with me.

If I fry a pork steak—not a nice, thick chop, but a thin, fatty blade steak—and then smoke a cigar, the combined aromas mingle to form a powerful memory trigger. One whiff and I am back in the living room at Grandma and Grandpa McKenzie's, lying on the carpet, watching *The Lawrence Welk Show*. Grandpa is in his big, green easy chair, reading *The Fort Wayne News-Sentinel*. Grandma is watching the show from her gray chair with the wooden arms carved like swans' heads. Lawrence and the boys are wheezing and bleating and, even though I can't stand the show, I feel warm and safe and most of all secure, knowing that I have a place in the world, and this is it.

And then, just as quickly as it came, the moment leaves me and I am once again a middle-aged man in a house in Indianapolis. A house that needs a window opened.

The smell of caramel corn. The smell of a hardware store—not a modern mega-giganto warehouse store, but a real hardware with wooden floors and nails in kegs. The smell of newsprint and ink. Each of these takes me back to someplace specific in my life—the dime store in LaGrange, the hardware store in Howe, the newspaper office where Dad worked. It only lasts for a second or two, but it is as real to me as if I had traveled back through time itself.

But the aroma that works most powerfully is that of onions and celery, generously peppered, sautéing in a skillet. One tiny whiff and I am a kid, lying in bed on a cold, dark November morning in northern Indiana, realizing as he awakes that it is Thanksgiving Day and his mother is already down in the kitchen preparing a feast.

I love Thanksgiving. The older I get, the more it means to me.

When I was a kid, Thanksgiving was mostly about food. It still is, to a great degree, but back then the meal was the highlight of the day.

It meant turkey, a bird we did not see on our table with regularity the way we do today. Now you can go to the store and buy an assortment of turkey parts all year long: legs, thighs, wings, breasts. You can buy ground turkey, turkey cutlets, turkey tenderloins. We eat it for the health benefits, of course—good old low-fat turkey, sitting there in the meat case, offering to spare us from heart attacks—and because the rules we used to go by are falling away, one by one.

Think about it. When I was a kid, my mother had a rule that said no soda pop before 3 PM. And she was not alone in this. Most of the kids I knew were subject to the same rule. We envied the kid on our block whose mom let them have a bottle (and it was always bottles, never cans in those days) of Coke at 10 AM on a Saturday. *Wow,* we thought. *Ol' Herbie is living the good life for sure.*

Most homes had one TV, and most TV sets picked up three channels, four or five in the urban areas. In our case, it was more like two and a half. We got three channels from South Bend—Channel 16, Channel 22 and Channel 28—but we never got clear pictures from all three on the same night. If 16 and 22 were coming in, 28 would be all snowy. If 22 and 28 were clear, the picture from 16 would be full of weird diagonal lines. If 16 and 28 were strong, we would get sound but no picture from 22. And it was never the same two nights in a row.

That meant Mom had to set up rules about how we watched television—who got to pick the channels, how much we got to watch, and so on. And then we were given to understand that all rules were off if Dad was watching. When Dad watched TV, he was in charge of the channel selector, and that was that. No arguments.

Now, it seems, we have TVs in practically every room of our

houses—bedrooms, kitchen, even out in the garage—and each person can choose from among a million channels and watch it twenty-four hours a day on his or her own personal set. The only TV that doesn't seem to get much of a workout is the one in the family room, because nobody can agree on what to watch.

Well, it used to be that way with turkey. You'd go for most of a year and never see it, and then come November and December you'd have two turkey dinners, Thanksgiving and Christmas, in the span of a month. Then it was another eleven months before you saw that magnificent bird again.

Actually, I think it was the waiting that made it magnificent. You eat turkey often enough and you begin to see that it's really sort of an undistinguished bird. Duck and goose have more flavor. Chicken requires far less work. Turkey, it dawns on you, is overrated. Or overexposed. Garrison Keillor, a wise man, wrote that if you limit yourself to one turkey a year, it is a powerful experience. I know what he means. I had those powerful experiences every November of my kidhood.

※ ※ ※

It's dark and cold, but when I poke my nose out from under the covers it tells me that Mom already is at work in the kitchen. I smell onions and celery sautéing in butter. Mom's making the stuffing for today's Thanksgiving dinner. I know that if's she's at the stuffing-making stage of the game, she's about a third of the way through the meal. For Mom, making the stuffing is actually sort of a breather in a long morning of cooking and baking.

I tumble out of bed, put on my jeans and boots, and make my way to the kitchen. I'm one of those kids who always wakes up hungry anyway, who rushes through his morning chores so he can get to that cereal bowl, and the smell of a Thanksgiving dinner in the works just makes my morning hunger all the more acute.

Mom is wielding the pepper shaker over the sauté pan as I arrive. She inherited from her mother a heavy hand with the pepper shaker.

Fried eggs come to the table generously flecked with black at Grandma's house, and they were precisely the same at ours. Hard-boiled eggs, for some reason, were even more highly seasoned. When my mother gets done peppering a hard-boiled egg, it looks like a lump of coal.

I look around the kitchen to see all that Mom had done in the wee hours. Pies—two pumpkin, one mince, one apple—are cooling on the counter. A big bowl of bread dough, eventually to be rolled into cloverleaf biscuits, is rising under a towel on the back of the stove. And out on the back porch, in the chill of the morning, I can see all kinds of salads—vegetable salads, fruit salads, gelatin salads—glittering like gems in their glass bowls.

And sitting on the kitchen table, all pink and rubbery, its legs open and its wings tucked back under its shoulders, is the turkey, a twenty-pounder bought fresh the day before from Booth's Poultry Farm, over by the Steuben County Line.

"Do your chores, eat your breakfast and then stay out of the kitchen," Mom orders.

I clomp down to the cellar and attend to the furnace. That job is mine and mine alone. It's a stoker furnace, the kind that uses pieces of coal the size of a throat lozenge. You shovel the coal into a hopper and an auger carries it into the firebox. Keeping the auger full, the fire stoked and the box free of clinkers is my responsibility and I feel very grown-up, at fifteen years old, to scoop the coal from the bin and dump it into the hopper. I imagine I am shoveling coal on a steamship, making its way across the North Atlantic. Opening the door and poking into the firebox with a long, iron pole, I am in the mills in Gary, getting ready to pour hissing, glowing, molten steel into forms to make ingots. And reaching in with tongs to take out the clinkers, I am . . . well, I am a kid in northern Indiana reaching in with tongs to take out the clinkers. I don't have a good fantasy for taking out the clinkers. I wish I had. Clinkers are a pain in the butt, the part of furnace chores I hate most.

There are animals to be fed, pets and livestock both. We keep, at various times, geese, chickens, ducks, rabbits, goats, feeder calves and later Amy's Shetland pony, Peaches, as foul-tempered a beast that ever walked on four legs. The rule, as on all farms, is that the animals eat their breakfast before you do.

Chores finished, I wolf down a bowl of Cheerios while Mom continues to work in the kitchen, mixing the onions and celery with cubed bread, dousing it with broth made from the turkey's neck and giblets, mixing in a couple of eggs, and adding seasoning: sage, powdered garlic, salt and, of course, more pepper. Then she begins spooning it carefully into the cavity of the bird.

"Finish up and get out of here," Mom says without looking up. I put my bowl in the sink and make my way to the living room to see if the Thanksgiving Day parade is on TV. If it is, I'll go upstairs and awaken my baby sister, Amy. She loves parades, the Macy's parade especially, and doesn't want to miss a moment.

Amy and I sit together on the sofa—she in her nightie with a bowl of Cap'n Crunch in her lap—and watch parades all morning. And as the day wears on, the smells from the kitchen change from onion and celery to the glorious aroma of a turkey roasting. When Mom opens the oven door to baste it, you can hear it sputtering. Then, a few seconds behind the sound, comes a blast of warm air carrying the scent of that turkey and making us so hungry we can hardly stand it.

Amy and I are joined in the living room by P.D. and Dad. Vicky is pressed into service in the kitchen with Mom, peeling potatoes white AND sweet, scrubbing vegetables, trying to stay ahead of the mountain of dishes and utensils piling up in the sink. Occasionally, we boys are called to the kitchen for dish-drying duty. We don't mind. To be in the kitchen is to be closer to that turkey, and we can fill our noses at least, if not our stomachs.

At about 1:00 PM, Mom pokes her head through the kitchen doorway. "Mike! P.D.!" she barks. "I need you to set up the table." We tear ourselves away from the television set and tug apart the big Duncan Phyfe dining table. I fetch the leaves from behind the breakfront and align them carefully on the rails. Then P.D. and I squeeze the table back together.

Mom immediately places upon it a felt-backed pad and a table-cloth of ivory brocade. Then Vicky and Amy set it—the good plates, the good silver, the good drinking glasses. At each place is a folded cloth napkin, made of the same fabric as the tablecloth. This tells us—as if we didn't already know—that we were about to have a special meal. Most days we used paper napkins, or if those were gone and Mom hadn't yet been to the store, paper towels. Cloth napkins equal a feast.

At 1:30 PM, a car pulls into the driveway and out steps Grandma Redmond, Dad's sister, Aunt Susie with her husband, Uncle Marvin, and our one and only first cousin on that side, their son, David, whose age splits the difference between P.D.'s and mine. Aunt Susie and Grandma are toting dishes—green beans cooked with salt pork and a touch of onion, and creamed corn, which we never have at our house and which P.D. and I think is very exotic.

Hellos are exchanged and coats are taken. Grandma perches in a chair and asks us about school. Aunt Susie holds Amy in her lap. Dad and Uncle Marvin talk about man stuff—football, tire rotation, things like that. David joins P.D. and me in front of the TV.

And then a parade of food begins coming out of the kitchen: cut-glass dishes filled with olives, black and green, and celery sticks. Plates of cheese. The vegetables, five or six varieties. All those glittering salads. A large mixing bowl heaped with mashed potatoes. Another bowl, almost as big, full of sweet potatoes. Yet another full of stuffing. A gallon or so of gravy. A basket with dozens and dozens of hot, home-made rolls.

And then, finally, the turkey: golden brown and magnificent.

We say grace—Grandma insists on it—and Dad walks into the kitchen for a knife and sharpening steel. After a few quick strokes, he thumbs the blade carefully to test the edge. Satisfied, he picks up a fork and begins to carve.

A leg comes off first. This makes me happy. It's mine. Everyone else in the family wants white meat, but I'm a turkey leg man all the way. Not only do I prefer the taste, I like having a giant club of meat upon which to gnaw. It makes me feel like Henry VIII.

Dad carves off enough to get us started, and then the food starts coming around the table—meat and potatoes, vegetables and stuffing, salads and rolls and relishes—even with the big plates, there isn't room for it all. You have to make choices—regular potatoes this time around, sweet potatoes when we start going for seconds.

Mom, as usual, is fretting. She always worries that the turkey will be overdone (it isn't) or that the stuffing will need more seasoning (it doesn't) or that she has forgotten something. That last one is usually true. At some point in the meal Mom is guaranteed to suddenly jump up from her chair with a gasp, run to the kitchen, and come back to the table bearing yet another vegetable or another salad. It never fails. This time it's a Jell-O salad, although nobody will notice it until dinner is over and P.D. sees it, sitting there forlornly on the back porch.

And so we feast. It's all so good that we can't stop ourselves, despite the admonishments to slow down or save room for pie. We have waited all year for this meal, and now that it's here we want to take in as much of it as we can.

The food comes around again and again—more potatoes, more stuffing, more gravy, more green beans, more creamed corn, more, more, more of everything. And the joy that we feel seems to grow with every service. We laugh and talk and steal food from each other's plates. Well, P.D. and David and I steal food from each other's plates. We knew better than to try that stunt with a grownup.

And then, when it seems like we can eat no more, Mom and Vicky and Aunt Susie begin taking up the dishes, hauling our feast back into the kitchen while we sit at the table and try to catch our breath.

Then they come back in with dessert.

This is what Uncle Marvin has been waiting for. He adores pumpkin pie, and by consensus my mother is considered to be one of northern Indiana's better pie bakers. As she cuts the pie and places it on serving plates, she asks the rest of us, "Small piece or large?" She never asks Uncle Marvin. She already knows the answer: large. Very large.

The mincemeat pie is for Vicky. She's one of those weird kids who likes spinach, liver and squash. Mincemeat pie, which P.D. and I think is an impossibly weird name for a dessert, is right up her alley. P.D. and I are convinced it can't be fit to eat. Not that we've ever tried it. We don't have to. With that name, we just know.

Another bowl comes around, heaped with whipped cream—real whipped cream, not the stuff from a can or some substitute made of vegetable oil and artificial dairy flavor. It is spooned in great clouds onto our pieces of pie. Then we set about achieving the impossible— packing dessert into stomachs where no room is left.

And then, dinner over, we rise groaning in twos and threes. The women go out to the kitchen to begin repairing the wreckage. Dad and Uncle Marvin settle themselves in the living room, soon to fall asleep in front of the football games. Amy goes upstairs to nap, and we boys go outside to stumble around, groggy from all that food, while recounting, in great detail, the meal we have just eaten—who had the most turkey, who tried the most different dishes, who accidentally put gravy on his cranberry sauce when he got a little carried away with the ladle.

And then we start counting the hours until suppertime, when we can start in on the leftovers.

※ ※ ※

That was Thanksgiving then, in my kidhood. It's much the same now, but with something added: the thanks.

We kids would always be asked what we were thankful for, and our answers would be kid answers: I'm thankful for my new bicycle. I'm thankful I got a good score on the spelling test. I'm thankful that Mike didn't beat me up when I knocked that model car off the dresser and broke it.

Now my answer is different. I am thankful for the life I have been given, for the friends I have made, for the way I have been allowed to find a way to make a living by doing what I love best. I am thankful for the bounty of food that appears on my table, not just on a Thursday in November, but every day.

And I am thankful that in most American homes, people are doing almost exactly what I do, without regard to race or color or religion. With all that makes us different, Thanksgiving is the one holiday that can bring us together, family by family. We gather together.

I am thankful for Thanksgiving itself.

⌐ Pineapples, Candles and the Three Wise Guys. ⌐

Christmas time is here. I hope we survive it . . .

I come from a family of Christmas nuts. I mean it. There is a streak of insanity running through the females to whom I am related, and it shows up every December.

Wait. Check that. It shows up in late November, as soon as the dishes are cleared from Thanksgiving dinner.

As the last dessert plate is taken to the sink, they begin dispatching children and husbands to their attics and garages to begin hauling in boxes of Christmas decorations. Holiday music begins playing on their stereos. And they begin the arduous task of turning their homes into something resembling a department-store Santa Land.

I am speaking of my two sisters, Vicky and Amy, who learned this behavior from their mother and are, at this minute, passing it along to their daughters.

In my house I have a Christmas tree. A tree. As in one. Singular.

In their houses, they have a Christmas tree . . . in every room. They have big trees in the living room. Smaller ones in the family room. Themed trees (angels, Winnie the Pooh, the entire collection of Hallmark Collector Ornaments Years 1995, 1996 and 1997) in their hallways. Miniature trees on the endtables. A tree for a dining room centerpiece. All crowded with hundreds of lights and an equal number of ornaments.

And that's just the beginning. On their mantels they hang stockings. Theirs. The kids. One for Grandma. Stockings for the dogs and cats. Stockings for dogs and cats they haven't seen in years. And a couple of extras they picked up at a Christmas shop last year because they looked cute.

Living room tables are cleared for collections of Santa figurines, for Nativity scenes, for brass sculptures of reindeer. Pictures come down from the walls, and in their place go Currier and Ives prints of horse-drawn sleighs gliding through deep, snowy forests.

From the kitchen come plates of candies and cookies, set about in various rooms of the house, each arranged perfectly and precisely, so that the moment a piece of peanut-butter fudge or a gingerbread man is eaten, it is immediately replaced with a fresh one just to restore the balance.

Like I said, these people are nuts.

Somehow, it skipped me. I like Christmas, and I like Christmas decorations, but I try to keep things modest. A nice tree, some nice ornaments, a few holiday knick-knacks here and there, just enough to put a little holiday spirit into the house. Less is more, I tell myself.

Or, as you have no doubt figured out by now, I still have issues relating to the Christmases of my kidhood, at least the decorating part.

We had rules about the Christmas tree. I'm not kidding. Rules.

The first and most important of these had to do with the lights. There could be no two lights of the same color next to each other in any direction—across, up-and-down or diagonally. Given the shape of our trees—we favored eight-footers, short-needled, on the slender side—and the limited selection of colors available for Christmas lights in those days (red, blue, green, orange, white) you can see that having a tree without two lights of the same color next to one another was clearly impossible.

Didn't matter. That was the rule, and we spent an awful lot of time, and burned an awful lot of fingertips, trying to follow it.

I have always credited my mother with this rule. In the years since Dad's death she has denied any responsibility. "That was your father's rule," she says. "I didn't care." Maybe so, but I can't recall my mother ever saying, "Oh, Pat, knock it off. It doesn't matter if we have two red ones next to each other."

Whoever rule it was, I find it interesting that Mom's Christmas trees have now lights of only one color: white.

The second rule involved ornaments. We boys were given to understand that there were two classes of ornaments for the Christmas tree: good ones, and the ones that we could handle. Good ones were entrusted only to the careful hands of Dad, Mom and Vicky.

This rule came into being the year my brother and I got pop guns for Christmas. They were splendid pop guns, made to look like Kentucky long rifles, nearly as tall as we were, perfect for the days when we played Daniel Boone, Davy Crockett, or *Last of the Mohicans* (my grandfather's favorite book and thus a part of our library whether we wanted it or not). The guns fired cork balls, about the size of a marble, propelled by a cap placed on the firing pan.

It was about noon on Christmas Day when my brother P.D. found himself unable to resist the Don't-Shoot-Those-Things-in-the-House rule. He rammed a cork ball into the barrel, put a cap in place, and aimed for a Christmas ornament.

As luck—bad luck—would have it, he chose one of Mom's very favorites: an old glass pineapple, a full seven inches from top to bottom, hand-blown in Czechoslovakia.

My brother had not at this time studied physics. Heck, I don't think he had even studied fractions. Therefore, you can see he was flawed in his reasoning when he decided the light weight of the cork ball could do no real damage. He fully expected it to hit the pineapple and bounce to the floor.

He propped his gun on a sofa cushion, sighted down the barrel, and squeezed the trigger. His aim was true. The cork ball rocketed across the living room, hit the pineapple dead-center, and smashed it into a million pieces.

This is when we learned of our mother's extraordinary powers of hearing. She was out in the kitchen, preparing dinner. There was a mixer going. The phone was ringing. Out in the living room we had the TV on and Christmas music playing on the radio.

And through all that din my mother heard the sound of an ornament breaking. Not only that, she knew by the sound exactly WHICH ornament.

Boy, was she mad.

P.D. had his gun taken away for two weeks. And even though I had nothing to do with what happened, I was judged guilty by association—I, too, was a boy with a cork gun and therefore not to be trusted—and from that day on, we weren't even allowed to get NEAR any of the good Christmas ornaments.

Our job was to place the glass balls, the ones that were seventy-nine cents a dozen, on all the parts of the tree where Vicky thought it was too icky and scratchy. In other words, we worked on the back of the tree, squeezing ourselves in between the wall and the branches, while the rest of the family worked on the part of the tree you could actually see.

The final rule concerned tinsel, the shiny icicles that look like aluminum foil run through a paper shredder. Actually, there were two rules, Mom's and Dad's. Mom hated tinsel and Dad loved the stuff.

When all the ornaments had been placed, we would step back from the tree to admire it. "All done," Mom would say.

"Not quite," Dad would respond.

"Oh, Pat, not that godawful tinsel."

"Yes. It needs tinsel."

"Pat, you are not putting tinsel on that Christmas tree."

"Oh, yes I am."

We kids would just watch. We loved the annual tinsel fight. It was funny.

After an hour or so of debate, the folks would usually reach a compromise. Dad could put tinsel on the tree IF it was done carefully—one strand at a time, none of that throwing clumps of tinsel at the tree and letting gravity do the distribution.

Dad would do as ordered and finally the tree would be finished and the tinsel debate would be over. Sort of.

What really happened was that the folks changed their arguments from words to action. Dad would invariably sneak down in the middle of the night to put some more tinsel on the tree. Mom would get up the next morning and start taking it off. Dad would do it again the following night. Mom would follow suit the next morning. And it went on like this right up until Christmas morning.

We had a Christmas morning rule that said the youngest child should be the first to see the tree with all the presents arrayed beneath it. We would assemble at the top of the stairs and Dad would go down to plug in the tree and give everything one final check. When he gave the all-clear, we would troop down the stairs in reverse birth order.

Incidentally, since P.D. and I are the closest in age of any of the siblings, I only got to be first down the stairs for two Christmases. Vicky had four Christmases of her own before I came along, and P.D. got to be first for nine years—NINE YEARS—until Amy's birth knocked him out of the pole position. Life can be so unfair.

I am pretty sure that one of the things Dad did while we were all upstairs waiting was take advantage of one last tinsel opportunity. On Christmas mornings, there always seemed to be a few more clumps of shiny stuff on the tree. Mom would notice and say something about it, but Dad always played innocent and told her Santa Claus must have put them there.

That my brother is a Christmas nut is a little surprising to me. Christmas decorations figured in a traumatic episode of his kidhood, and you would think he'd have some sort of adult complex because of it. Not so. I guess Christmas nut-ism trumps trauma.

One December, when he was about ten, my brother saw in a hardware store window a decoration called angel chimes. It was a small tower, made of pressed brass. Around its base were four candleholders, a red candle in each. At the top was a fan, like that of a windmill placed horizontally. The fan drove a shaft to which were affixed four brass angels, each holding a clapper. Beneath them were four brass bells. As warm air rose from the burning candles, it turned the fan, which turned the shaft, which caused the angels to go round and round.

The clappers would strike the bells with a steady ding-ding-ding racket which somehow was supposed to say "Christmas."

Well, P.D. fell in love with these angel chimes and pestered Mom until she broke down and bought them. He brought them home and announced that they were HIS angel chimes, his own personal Christmas ornament, and that none of the rest of us were allowed to touch them, which suited us fine. Vicky and I thought they were dopey.

Every night that Christmas season, we lived our lives to the accompaniment of P.D.'s angel chimes. They ding-ding-dinged through supper. They ding-ding-dinged while we were trying to watch TV or doing our homework. He even attempted to bring them into our bedroom so they could ding-ding-ding us to sleep (his idea) but I put my foot down on that one.

It was Christmas morning, and among the bounty under the tree was an Emenee chord organ for P.D.—a cheap, wheezy, plastic thing that allowed people with limited skills to make something resembling music. The right hand would pick out a melody on a standard keyboard, while the left could choose accompaniment from a bank of chord buttons, white ones for the major chords, black ones for the minors.

P.D. played the thing all day and by evening had gotten good enough to play "An English Country Garden"—the first song in the book that came with the organ—at a tempo slightly slower than your average funeral dirge. The chord changes were holding him up. In P.D.'s hands, what was intended to be a sprightly little tune about flowers and sunshine sounded like something sung by people breaking rocks in a labor camp in Siberia.

The Emenee chord organ had a volume lever, but its design didn't really give you the full range of options from *pianissimo* to *fortissimo*. Basically, it went from silent to loud with no stops in between. This bothered P.D., who was looking for a dramatic way to end his funereal interpretation of "An English Country Garden." What he had in mind was to hold the final chord and have it fade out.

He discovered that if he turned off the organ while holding the chord, the little fan inside that blew air past the reeds would give him precisely the effect he was going for. As it slowed down, it executed a long, slow fade. The only trouble was, if he had one hand on a chord button and the other hand holding down a key, he couldn't get to the switch. Lifting a hand would ruin the effect.

And then he discovered that he could lean over, keeping both hands in place, and turn off the organ with his nose. Voila. Fade-out, just like he intended.

That evening he was treating us to yet another slow, tortured rendition of "An English Country Garden" and, because it was evening, I suppose, he placed his angel chimes atop the organ. It was quite a contrast in tempo—the plodding tones of my brother's playing accompanied by the rapid ding-ding-ding of those chimes.

As he got to the end of the song, a full seven or eight minutes after he started, he leaned over and hit the off switch with his nose. Then he sat up and listened as the song faded to nothing.

He also heard a crackling noise, which he assumed was one of us shelling peanuts. Not so. In fact, he had gotten a little too close to the candles when he bent over to turn off the organ with his nose. His hair was on fire.

He sat there, smiling at his accomplishment, while a little leaf of flame danced upward from his head. Dad saw it immediately. He got up from his chair and walked across the room. As he passed my brother, he smacked him smartly atop the head with an open hand and put out the fire. Then he continued into the kitchen, all without saying a word.

P.D. sat there, stunned. He looked at me.

"Wow," he said. "Dad must really hate that song."

※ ※ ※

My family of Christmas nuts is exceedingly fond of tradition. Certain ornaments MUST be on the tree or it isn't finished (a status enjoyed by Mom's pineapple until P.D. shot it). Certain foods must be served (Mexican wedding cakes, fruitcake, and Mom's homemade chocolate-caramel-and-pecan turtles). And certain decorations must be on display, not the least of which is the Nativity set.

Mom has two Nativities. The big one has fancy hand-painted figures—the kind that make it look as though people in the Holy Land at the time of Jesus' birth were, in fact, Renaissance Italians who had moved there for the winter—blond in some cases, and all in those awkward Renaissance-painting poses of adoration, arms close to their sides, hands up, palms turned outward, that always looked to me like someone had just given them a sharp shove from behind.

The smaller Nativity is the family favorite, though. It's a tiny little cardboard stable. A cardboard star, covered with blue glitter, has a tab on the bottom and fits into a slot in the roof. On the back wall is a little hole through which you can run a Christmas light. And inside the stable are three little porcelain figurines—the Mary, Joseph and baby-Jesus-in-a-manger action figures.

Dad bought the nativity set for $1.79 at a Sears store on the way home from work one night in 1960. He set it up, stood back for us to admire it, and was shocked at our reaction. We didn't like it.

It wasn't complete, we told him. You can't have a manger scene unless you have wise men on camels bearing gold, frankincense and myrrh. Everybody knows that. And nothing would do, we told Dad, but that we get some guys on camels around the manger scene, pronto.

Dad went back out to look for them. Sears was closed so he went to a drugstore where he found a set of three plastic figurines of men on camels. They were shiny chrome except for the camel's saddle blankets. One was pink, one was blue and the third was green.

He brought them home and set them up. It didn't matter that they were in a different scale from the rest of the nativity, or that their chrome-plated garishness stood out in sharp contrast to the rest of the scene. They were guys on camels, and we kids were satisfied.

Vicky, the oldest, announced that she liked the pink one best, and that it would be her wise man on a camel. I followed suit and claimed the blue one.

This left the green one—the ugliest color by far—for P.D., who was annoyed.

111

"Hey!" he said. "How come I gotta get the green wise guy?"

And that is why, when we tell the Christmas story in our house, the birth of the baby Jesus is attended by the Three Wise Guys: Balthazar, Melchior and Phil.

I think back to the Christmases of my kidhood and, after I pick through the memories closest to the surface—the Christmas music we liked, the great presents we received, the embarrassing presents we gave one another (one year, when my piggy bank was empty, I gave my family postcards I had picked up on our trip to Florida a few months earlier)—I get to the deeper, more satisfying memories.

Dad and Mom had a rule that said we didn't go out to visit people, and neither did people come to visit us, on Christmas Day. Unlike other holidays, Christmas was reserved for us, and us alone. It was our day to be together, as a family.

Because of that, I remember Christmas as the one day of the year when we were a family in the best sense of the word. All our conflicts and disagreements and squabbles that on the other 364 days of the year made life so interesting—fun, sometimes, and difficult other times, but always interesting—did not exist on Christmas. It was a peaceful day, a quiet and gentle day, a joyous day filled with love. Each child felt loved, felt secure, felt safe in knowing that he had a place in this world and people who looked out for him, and at this moment it was wrapped around him like a soft, warm blanket.

I can't blame anyone for being nutty about a day like that. I guess, in my own way, I am a Christmas nut, too.

Afterword

·- Back to the Beginning. -·

Or, trying to make some sense out of all of this . . .

For the last few years, I have been lucky to make my living telling
stories, more often than not about my family. I didn't start out to
do that. I had a newspaper column to write, and it was supposed to be
funny, and sometimes the things I remembered from kidhood were far
funnier than anything I could find to make fun of in the news. And so
I told stories about growing up in Indiana as part of a big, rambunctious family.

Pretty soon, I became aware that I was not alone. Readers who
saw these stories began sending me stories about their own rambunctious families, and I soon learned that something I had always believed—that we Redmonds were somehow different from the American Family Norm—was, in fact, untrue. Every family is a nutball family in its own way. Each family may be unique in its quirks and foibles,
but it still gets down to the fundamental truth that families are basically goofy, and in that lies their charm and their genius.

I learned something else too: family means more to me than I
knew.

Despite the knocks—and there were a few—I grew up knowing
that I was loved, that I had a place in this world, and that there would
always be people to whom I can turn in times of need: my family.

I just hope I can still turn to them after they read this thing.

I have been told that what I do helps promote family values. That's nice if it's true, but that's not my objective. I have found over the years that whenever someone uses the words "family values," he or she usually means "my values," and while they may be perfectly good values, I don't believe in the one-size-fits-all approach.

There are all kinds of families out there, and you know what? I think most of them have pretty good values. I'm optimistic that way. I think most people try to make the right choices and do the right thing. And they do this, sometimes, against incredible odds.

Rather than promote family values, I hope my stories help people do what I believe to be the right thing: value families.